SUBSCRIPTIONS

SCINTILLA 16 and all later issues can be purchased through Amazon.com or Amazon.co.uk.
For convenience, we hope to make back issues available through Amazon in future.
Issues 1-15 are available directly from The Vaughan Association.
Please email **subscriptions@vaughanassociation.org** to get further details.

*

WEBSITE

www.vaughanassociation.org

EMAIL

subscriptions@vaughanassociation.org

Submissions for *Scintilla 22*

Please submit critical articles on literature in the metaphysical tradition to prose@vaughanassociation.org.

Please submit new poetry for consideration to poetry@vaughanassociation.org.

All submissions are peer reviewed

SCINTILLA

The Journal of the Vaughan Association

21

Magic is nothing els but the *Wisdom* of the *Creator* revealed and planted in the *Creature*.

Thomas Vaughan,
'Magia Adamica'

And after all the coyl of Academical licenciated Doctors, he onely is the true Physician, created so by the light of Nature, to whom Nature her selfe hath taught and manifested her proper and genuine operations by Experience.

Henry Vaughan,
'Hermetical Physick'

A journal of literary criticism, prose and new poetry
in the metaphysical tradition

Published by
The Vaughan Association

Published in 2018
Scintilla is a publication of The Vaughan Association

Some of the essays in each issue of *Scintilla* originate in talks first given at The Vaughan Association's annual Colloquium held over the last full weekend in April near the Vaughans' birth-place at Newton Farm near Llansantffraed, Breconshire.

ISBN-13: 978-1984980274
ISBN-10: 1984980270
ISSN 1368-5023

Published with the financial support of the Welsh Books Council

Typeset in Wales by the Dinefwr Print & Design, Rawlings Road, Llandybïe, Carmarthenshire, SA18 3YD
Printed by CreateSpace, USA

Contents

Preface

In *Scintilla 21* we continue this journal's tradition of exploring and extending the literary legacy of the Vaughan brothers and their literal and figurative poetic peers. These identical twins, who were shaped by the beauty of Breconshire from their youth, continually returned to their memories of the Usk river valley with its unique features: gently rolling hills and dense groves filled with flora and fauna, stones and rivers, history and myths. This landscape ignited their imaginations, as they sought to endure the social and political changes that swirled around them in seventeenth-century England. Their experiences with the horror of civil unrest, the erasure of familiar political and religious institutions, the struggle to retain identity and continuity, all marked these writers and their works. As Henry and Thomas reinvented themselves (Henry as 'Silurist' and Thomas as 'Eugenius Philalethes'), their creative works explored the relationships among identity, adversity, and the creative processes in their writing. *Scintilla* continues that tradition of probing these conjunctions and crossing boundaries between past and present; between place and vision; between our physical environment and our inner lives; between metaphysical experiences and the concrete language of science, poetry and healing.

We are honored that Dr. Rowan Williams opens this issue with a consideration of the relationship between Henry Vaughan's poetry and his twin brother Thomas' cosmology. In his exploration of the definition of the metaphysical, Williams reveals the Vaughan brothers' ability to help the soul "grow as it ought" and see "what it should." In a similar vein, Robert Wilcher examines the arc of Henry Vaughan's poetic development to explain what kind of poet Vaughan strove to be and what kind of reality he proffers in his poetry. Wilcher's analysis suggests that in his rejection of Jonsonian tradition, Vaughan transitions to a poetry of faith, marked by his belief that the indwelling of the Holy Spirit is what makes it possible for the Christian poet to create art. Honoring Welsh poetry has served as a foundational element of this journal's mission, and Sean McDowell participates in that tradition through his detailing the influence of the Welsh poetic heritage on Henry Vaughan's poetry. McDowell dispels the myth that many of Vaughan's poems demonstrate an architectural instability. Through his technical analysis of Vaughan's images and rhyming patterns, McDowell highlights the poet's careful attention to linguistic detail, his deep sensitivity to verbal sounds, and layers of introspection as markers of his close ties to the Welsh bardic tradition. In the spirit of associating Henry Vaughan with his poetic peers, Jonathan Naumann investigates the means by which Vaughan reinvents images, employs devotional pastiche, and sublimates poetic excellence to devotional discipline in his efforts to emulate the work of George Herbert.

It is an abiding interest of *Scintilla* to explore the relation between the writer and the often very physical processes of the creative process. Michael Durrant helps the reader mine that relationship as he traces the production, circulation, and appropriation of Charles I's *Eikon Basilike*. This text was reputed to often be bound in fragments of Charles' own bloody clothing, a textual phenomenon of print culture that links physical texts and human life in inextricable ways. Jeremy Hooker suggests that David Jones' engagement with concrete tactile elements of the natural world provide the means by which the poet may maintain his "creaturely" status, while simultaneously opening access to the order of another, transcendent world. From this perspective, Jones, in highlighting the details of our modern earth and engagement with the life sciences, not only crafts poems as signs of our status as human creatures, but also as means of directing us to look beyond those signs for a Creator.

As it has for the past decade, *Scintilla* continues to extend its reach exploring the variety of poets and thinkers who write in the metaphysical tradition. *Scintilla 21* offers important reflections, not only on poets such as Henry Vaughan and David Jones who have frequently been subjects of interest in our pages, but introduces a number of lesser known poetic voices.

Matthew Barton's poem in this issue follows the changing course and identity of the river Frome through South Gloucestershire and Bristol, observing the effects of the two-way relationship between flowing water and its changing environment. Barton's portrait of the Frome's varying incarnations within a single dynamic entity offers a purchase on the word currents brought together for *Scintilla* 21, in which a shared sense of the numinous flows through a multiplicity of engagements with disparate environments, from the 'station washroom or boutique hotel en-suite/ or dosshouse' to docklands, deserts, museums and a 'Tex-Mex joint'.

As ever in *Scintilla*, there is a suspicion of dogma; a genuinely speculative and receptive imagination plays freely in reinhabited pasts and in 'quantum futures[s]'. The pitfalls of the single view are avoided as poems strive to think across and between categories of experience, 'the way a bat hears/ the silhouette of trees' (as Eithne Lannon puts it) – synaesthesia of this kind being crucial to our ability to perceive what Ruth Bidgood calls 'the mingling of here and now/ with gone'. For this issue, the editors have responded to poems that do not shy away from the terror and trauma of our own, and others', 'fleshly durance', whether human or non-human. What Patrick Deeley experiences in front of a T-Rex skull in Ulster Museum is a confrontation with our own instinctive reptilian violence – a revelation linked to, not different from, Charles Wilkinson's vision of 'a series of ideas ris[ing] bright/ as babies from new fonts'. If Christopher Meredith's bird's-eye view of human finitude defies the gravity of rivers, trees and dinosaur bones, it reminds us too that viewpoints are the source of liabilities as well as revelations. The conceit of an aerial view asks us both to peel our eyes for glimpses of our 'half-seen gods', and to acknowledge our confinement as 'bottom-dwellers crawling in mud roads'.

Reflections on The Vaughan Brothers: Poetry meets Metaphysics

ROWAN WILLIAMS

Perhaps the single best-known line of Henry Vaughan is 'I saw Eternity the other night' – typical of the idiom which Vaughan borrows from Herbert, the casual, offhand, conversational introduction of profundity. But 'the other night' is not just a piece of stage-setting. Every reader of Henry Vaughan will be conscious of how pervasive in his poetry is the theme of *night*: thoughts and perceptions, changes in the life of the spirit, are possible at night in a way they are not in the light of day, and, in his best-known meditation on this subject, he sees the daylight as the generator of confusing, plural, uncontrollable perceptions and allurements:

> But living where the sun
> Doth all things wake, and where call mix and tyre
> Themselves and others, I consent and run
> To ev'ry myre;
> And by this world's ill guiding light,
> Erre more than I can do by night. (The Night)

For the mind and spirit to be illuminated by God's light, darkness is necessary, 'The day of spirits', the time when 'spirits their fair kinred catch': silence and the attentiveness that silence imposes open us up to communication from sources we should otherwise ignore. We are in touch with '*Christ's* progress and his prayer time':

> God's silent, searching flight;
> When my Lord's head is filled with dew, and all
> His locks are wet with the clear drops of night;
> His still, soft call;
> His knocking time; the soul's dumb watch,
> When spirits their fair kinred catch.

Night-time is when the poet turns from multiplicity to simplicity, from words to silence, from act to reception; and this 'dim' world of occluded sight, where the sheer variety of things is obscured, is, paradoxically, the context in which revelation occurs, the 'deep, but dazzling darkness' in which we see clearly who we are and who God is, speaking 'at mid-night . . . with the Sun', like Nicodemus in John chapter 3.[1] And, in another deployment of similar imagery in 'Cock-Crowing', we find the idea of seeds implanted during the night beginning to open up as day dawns – a genuine and interior illumination to keep us alert in the daytime to God's truth, and so to 'close the eye' to worldly illusion: 'where thou dost not close the eye/It never opens'. We live under clouds and veils, and God's light is needed to break or tear away this obstruction – 'O take it off! Make no delay!' So what we recognise at dawn is something of the process by which the 'light and heat' that pervades the universe (and which we habitually do not sense) enters our souls in the darkness and gradually 'unclothes' our worldly perceptions so that we see and feel what is veiled. As in 'Vanity of Spirit', we must learn to discern the weak residual gleams of insight in ourselves. But when we try to put these together in our own intellectual power, the light weakens and disappears. The 'eclips'd Eye' can only be restored by the 'disapparelling' of the soul, the death of the familiar. Dawn tells us to strip away interior darkness; exterior darkness gives us the opportunity of unveiling what we cannot see in our own light or the world's light.

But this leads us on to thinking further about what is communicated at night. It is the time when we see the stars; and for Vaughan these stars are in their way as important as the darkness itself. Thus, in 'Midnight', we read of what the nocturnal communication of spirits catching their kindred might amount to. Here are the stars working on us, streaming into our souls, working and winding:

> What Emanations,
> Quick Vibrations,
> And bright Stirs are there!

This contrasts with the sluggish and chilly 'Motions' that come from our own souls. Heaven is 'a firie-liquid light' (surely this particular seventeenth century Neoplatonic picture shaped the wonderful description of the warm luminosity of interstellar space in C.S. Lewis's *Out of the Silent Planet!*[2]), and the illumination and transformation of our chilly sublunar spirits comes from their

1 On Vaughan's pre-Romantic revaluation of night, see also Shimon Sandbank, 'Henry Vaughan's Apology for Darkness,' *Studies in English Literature*, 7 (1967), pp. 141-152.

2 C.S. Lewis, *Out of the Silent Planet* (New York: Macmillan, 1967 [1938]), pp. 28-30.

reception of this stream of heavenly life: the fiery light of heaven kindles the 'bloud And water' of our souls, uniting 'in one beame', so that the 'liquors' of our humanity will 'burne and streame'. The same theme can be found in 'The Lampe', where the 'firie thread' from the stars finds its way downwards to the human soul (Vaughan compares the light to that of a glow-worm, a frequent presence in his nocturnal poems). The lamp of the title points to the light and heat of the stars kindling the soul, and the melting wax or tallow, with its 'warm droppings' adds the element of penitent tears. When the lamp goes out, oil and fire are both exhausted; but for the soul, when it is 'out', that is, when it has exited from its earthly imaginings and self-centred habits, the real life of devotion begins: 'whensoe're I'm out, both shal be in, /And where thou mad'st an end, there I'll begin.' Behind this image lies the general principle which Vaughan shared with the entire Platonist and Hermetic world of his day, the conviction that there was a consonance and mutual attraction between what was above and what was below: so the light of the stars is drawn down towards us and we are drawn up to and into it. God's Spirit has been planted, 'a sacred ray', in us, yet we have allowed our own fleshly energy to stifle its proper growth ('Repentance'); I must turn to the signs of God's grace in the world at large, to 'All that have signature or life' (an important allusion to the common doctrine of the intelligible signs of God's presence in creation), while also acknowledging that my habitual sinfulness needs the specific action of divine forgiveness before it can be released to see fully and clearly. The soul is journeying and questing, combining its consistent penitence with growing attention to the signs of God around, and so becoming more receptive to the fire and light that is streaming from heaven towards us, and which is so vividly embodied in the stars at night. 'The Search', one of Vaughan's more ambitious poems, imagines dawn breaking after a night of 'roving *Extasie*', as I set out 'To find my Saviour': the poet reviews the whole of sacred history, finding Christ always having moved on before him, and at last confidently declaring, 'The Sun's broke through to guide my way' – only to hear, in a spare, song-like passage, a voice telling him to look inside, not outside, in 'another world' which is no longer 'out of Doores'. Behind this (as in 'The Night') is the hallowed imagery of the Song of Songs, the quest for the beloved and the interrogation as to where he has gone ahead; but this is also developed by St Augustine in Books VII and X of the *Confessions*, a text whose echoes in Vaughan deserve more study – and indeed in the contemplative poetry of St John of the Cross. Augustine declares, 'You [God] were within and I was in the external world and sought you there'[3]; Vaughan's search has ultimately to lead away even from the earthly sites of God's action in revelation to

3 *Confessions*, ed. by H. Chadwick, ed. (Oxford: Oxford University Press, 1991), X.27.

the inner world. Once again, the light of this world's sun is shown to be illusory, dispersing the concentration of the spirit; only when this is hidden can we see plainly.

'The Morning-Watch' sums all this up vividly: 'The pious soul by night/ Is like a clouded starre', its light shining 'above', abiding in God, so that, when its usual perception is overlaid by sleep and darkness, it is in fact more exposed to heaven. 'Dew' falls all night so that at dawn 'shoots of glory' may appear as we wake. Briefly, as light appears, all things are in harmony: 'Prayer is/ the world in tune', and this harmony is felt as the legacy of what has been communicated during the hours of darkness. Like the stars in their own heavenly order, characterised by 'Silence and light and watchfulness' ('The Constellation'), the soul begins to reflect the harmony that is above, becoming 'more and more in love with day' as it turns away from the false light of human will and earthly greed.

It is, all in all, a powerful family of images, elaborating a basic paradox in the work of Vaughan and of many writers on contemplation: what we think of as night is the source of illumination; what we think of as daylight is a distracting and dispersing atmosphere which occludes our real nature and impedes the growth of those seeds implanted in darkness, those kindlings of the Spirit in us that are activated by the heat and light of the stars when we learn to look heavenwards at night-time. But the interest of this imagery is not only a matter of what Vaughan does in a wide variety of poems (the passages quoted here could be paralleled many times over); the language of stars and heavenly light reflects, as already noted, a particular cosmology – and one to which Vaughan's twin brother Thomas made a very distinctive contribution. It is impossible that Vaughan was unaware of his brother's speculations; and some of his imagery is clarified still further if we read it alongside Thomas's texts. These are not the easiest reading, it has to be said. In Thomas's own lifetime, they were a byword for arbitrary and fanciful refinements on Neoplatonic themes; and he himself was obstinately unwilling to look for any convergence with other and more sophisticated thinkers. Querulous, hypersensitive and rude, he could be as abusive about a fellow Platonist like Henry More as he was about Oxford Aristoteleans of his day; his eclecticism is shown in borrowings from Paraclesus, Cornelius Agrippa, the Cabbalistic Zohar and assorted hermeticist sources. Yet he has flashes of his brother's vividness and concreteness, and has a distinct facility in coining memorable technical terms for his abstruse notions ('tiffany' for 'theophany' is the best-known instance[4]). And he is especially concerned with ideas of the seed of light in the soul and its relation with the light of heaven and the stars.

4 *The Works of Thomas Vaughan*, ed. by A. Rudrum (Oxford: Clarendon Press, 1984), p. 305.

Thomas Vaughan's *Anima Magica Abscondita* speaks of 'a spiritual, metaphysical grain, a seed or glance of light' as the centre of the soul[5]; a seed of light which is habitually like 'a *Candle* shut up in a dark-Lanthorn' (as his *Anthroposophia Theomagica* puts it, in a phrase strongly reminiscent of Henry's 'The Lamp'),[6] and which we need to have unveiled,[7] just as in Henry's 'Cock-Crowing'. But the parallels go further. Thomas's cosmology involves the imagery of divine light steadily compressing darkness; out of this friction and compression, a 'thin' spiritual substance is squeezed out of the material world, and is then kindled into fire by the heat and light of God. Creation begins when light itself posits darkness, brings into being its own opposite so as to become one element among others in a universe rather than a self-sufficient eternal reality. This is the 'first separation' from which all finite life eventually flows; but the distinctive life of the various levels of created being result from the process by which the divine Spirit extracts from the darkness (through the pressure already described, pressure mediated by *aer agilis*, the subtle gas which expands into or against the darkness) the 'thin' created light which flows upwards into the visible heavens. This is both light and 'upper water', the 'interstellar sky' in which the fire of the stars burns[8] – Henry's 'firie-liquid' medium. 'The stars are resident with us', writes Thomas, and we have 'astronomy under our feet'.[9] The pressure of divine Spirit upon this earth is making it harder and brighter: the heavenly 'water' transmits purifying fire to the earth to make it more starlike. The jewels found in the depths of the earth are signs of this pressure at work, compacting cruder and less formally organised material into what is luminous and precious. Part of this same process, however, is a sort of reversal of the pressure, whereby earth's impure waters are sucked up by the attraction of the heavens, condensed or compressed once again and returned in rain. The parallel here is with Henry's 'The Showre': the 'drowsie Lake' breathes forth its impurities which are sucked up from above and allowed to fall back in repentant tears; so with the soul, lazy and imperfect breathings of prayer can still be purified by love and grace and turned towards genuine penitence, so that tears fall and make soft the heart's earth. Divine action thus both hardens and softens the earth, pressing down to intensify its fiery brightness, moistening it to allow seeds to germinate. As in Henry's poetry, so in Thomas's cosmology, fire and water are imagined together as the medium through which air presses down upon earth, both compacting it and drawing it closer to the state of fiery liquidity which is the life of the stars.

5 Ibid., p. 111.
6 Ibid., p. 81.
7 Ibid., p. 76.
8 Ibid., p. 61.
9 Ibid., p. 64.

So as God's Spirit moves on the lower waters of creation, it does so through the 'moyest, silent Fire' which accompanies his presence[10]; this fire presses upon us so as to reunite us with the light above, thus drawing back upwards the created spirit which has fallen into the dark illusoriness of this earth, 'the body's night'[11] – a phrase deriving ultimately from the Zohar, by way of Pico della Mirandola. The body is a garment, indeed a 'Lanthorn', the covering for light, necessary within the lower realm but destined to be taken away, dissolved in the heat and light of increasingly direct divine encounter. As in Henry's poetry, once again, we have a stress upon the need for a radical stripping away of the outer world and its impressions – not because this is a world of evil; we need the body as a vehicle for perception and testing. But without divine grace we are left without a co-ordinating vision which allows us to see beyond the diversity of worldly impressions; the plurality of the material world has to be obscured for us to grasp the unity of the world above.

Both Vaughan brothers share the same fundamental cosmology: human beings contain a divine seed of light or fire, and, as with the whole of this lower creation, they stand in need of divine action, divine pressure, in order for this seed to grow as it should. That divine pressure both softens the heart in repentance and strengthens the heart to become more light-bearing – as is the case in the lower universe as a whole. Divine action is mediated by heat and light, and by water and fire together, the medium in which the heavenly bodies exist; so the stars above are both images of the renewed soul and agents of its renewal. The contemplation of their beauty and order opens up the soul to a true and active influence.

> O what bright quickness,
> Active brightness,
> And celestial flowes,
> Will follow after,
> On that water
> Which thy Spirit blowes! ('Midnight')

None of this is simply to argue that Henry Vaughan accepted or even understood every feature of his brother's idiosyncratic cosmology; his use of the imagery cannot be mapped with exactitude onto Thomas's systems. But there is enough to show that he certainly uses Thomas's scheme to *think with* – as one would expect from a poet, who is always going to be doing a lot more than versifying a system. Attention to Thomas's speculations, though, helps us see

10 Ibid., p. 65.
11 Ibid., p. 81: '*in noctem corporis.*'

more clearly some of what is most distinctive about Henry in the world of seventeenth century poetry. His oddity is easy to miss if we simply read him alongside the other 'metaphysicals'. The fact is that he belongs emphatically to the mid-century, to the world that produced Traherne on the one hand and the foundation of the Royal Society on the other, the world of anti-Aristotelean reaction, fascination both with empirical observation and with vaguely occult wisdom (often in some tension with each other: it is always worth remembering that Isaac Newton, some twenty years younger than Vaughan, was looked at askance in some circles for introducing into empirical science an 'occult' force like gravity). Donne and Herbert, with whom he is so readily bracketed in the textbooks, belong to an older intellectual world. Donne is still profoundly an Aristotelean: his philosophy and theology are on the whole unreconstructedly mediaeval, even when he uses as he habitually does tropes and concepts from that world in outrageous and unfamiliar ways. He is someone whose intellectual framework remains largely that of more than half a century earlier; the originality of his genius comes partly in his ability to inhabit it with a degree of irony, and to play so very creatively with its themes – being, as he was in so many ways, both insider and outsider. Herbert stands in another intellectual and theological world again, far more Erasmian than mediaeval; he approved and annotated Ferrar's translation of Valdes, that last of the great Erasmians in European Catholic circles, and, like Erasmus and Valdes, is reticent about doctrine and theory. Even more ironic than Donne, he creates a sensibility that is both cool and at the same time capable of colloquial and passionate expression, at a distance from metaphysics and strict dogmatic terminology. Pragmatic and pastoral, the great poems comfortably inhabit a doctrinal territory with a mildly Calvinist ambience, but take their force from the twists and turns of the voice speaking – highly self-aware, both resentful and resigned and conscious of the constructive tension in that.

Vaughan is seriously unlike them in two central respects. He is fascinated by a speculative world alien to both of them; and he is consistently someone who observes landscape. Donne is an urban writer if ever there was one; Herbert may have been a country parson, but his sensibility is deeply social, rooted in the great house, the tavern, the domestic conversation – remotely, the university he had left behind. Vaughan has none of Herbert's psychological acuity, his ear for the unexpected turns of speech, but he makes up for it by his eye for the material environment, that proto-Romantic strain in him that has been so often noted. He is a poet of *place* in a way that is not true of either of his fellows. And he has grown up in a world that has left behind both Donne's scholastic framework and Valdesian humanist pragmatism. This is a world of open and violent doctrinal controversy, but also of fresh system-building, and to understand the Vaughan brothers is to recognise that we are on the far side of a certain kind of break.

But here is another paradox about Vaughan: his early writing, as in *Olor Iscanus*, is formally unadventurous; it is not until he has digested Herbert that he begins to play with what we might think of as 'metaphysical' idioms and techniques, risking more abrupt and unexpected stylistic devices (the interruption of inserted song, for instance, as in 'The Search', the Herbertian style of abrupt openings and endings with conspicuously uneven line lengths, and so on). In other words, while he is definitely a mid-century writer, part of his distinctiveness is his obvious intention to re-create Herbert's spiritual world in another place and time. This becomes all the more poignant a task after the Civil War; many have observed that part of what Vaughan is doing is to build a 'church in words' that will substitute for the destroyed or alienated church buildings that have been taken over or ruined by Commonwealth partisans. But it is also perhaps for this very reason that he looks beyond the resources of the world that has been lost and ventures into a new and problematic cosmology. The outer world of ecclesial and state politics has exploded in disastrous violence; the traditional landmarks have vanished. What 'sacred map' can now be constructed, when the sheer routine presence of the Church of England is no longer to be taken for granted? Part of the answer is that already there is an intellectual renaissance of sorts in the fast expanding scientific world of the mid-century – Thomas Vaughan's world and Thomas Traherne's, though neither is exactly an ideal early modern scientist (most early modern scientists, of course, were not ideal early modern scientists . . .). But what Henry Vaughan is trying to do is, it seems, to tackle the question of how to reinvent a tradition in a radically new idiom – in this case, a tradition of interior attentiveness and the disciplines of self-forgetting, when the most obvious historic forms are not available. He skilfully and lovingly creates what it is tempting but inadequate to call a pastiche of Herbert's rhythms and even vocabulary, his distinctive verbal/musical habits, as if to say, I am writing from within the world that Herbert knew. But at the same time, he turns our attention to the distant scene above and the distant scene within, painting on a canvas Herbert would not have known. His brother's 'astronomy under our feet', with its vivid linkage between the stars and the soul and its bold interweaving of the imagery of fire and liquid, allows him to bring into focus the condition of the soul against a cosmic background of a different colouring from Herbert's, let alone Donne's. If we are occasionally reminded of Kant's famous line about 'the starry heavens above and the moral law within'[12] as the signs of God, that would miss the intense

12 Immanuel Kant, *Critique of Practical Reason*, ed. by M. Gregor (Cambridge: Cambridge University Press, 1997), p. 133.

realism that Vaughan assumes in his writing: there is a genuine participatory relation between what is above and what is below, and the stars are not just objects to be contemplated but vehicles of divine communication – visible when other perceptions are clouded over, visible at night when the soul is fed and enlarged by fire from heaven, and by the dew, 'the clear drops of night' that soak Christ's locks.

'Stars are of mighty use', he writes ('Joy of my life!'). And the saints who are celebrated in the third stanza of that poem are those who have most fully received what the stars can convey. They 'light/Us into Bed', he says, with a moment of prosaic directness. And then this reverses into a cosmic metaphor:

A swordlike gleame
Kept man for sin
First *Out*: this beame
Will guide him *In*.

The poem points to the *sharp,* piercing light that characterises the stars, to recall that at our fall from grace, our expulsion from Eden, the glitter of the sword shone so as to keep us away – and, if we put this alongside an image in 'Man's Fall and Recovery', part of the effect of that expulsion from Eden was the loss of 'A traine of lights' which in paradise enabled us to see clearly. Prior to our restoration, all we have is 'One sullen beame', the knowledge of our fallenness and guilt; but now (returning to the text of 'Joy of my life!'), the achieved lives of grace that we look to are there to guide us in. The saints have themselves been guided by the 'firie-liquid' light of heaven, the 'moyest, silent Fire' in which God moves and through which God works, and they are now stars to us, showing how the mutual attraction of above and below has been fleshed out in the event of grace, the return of the exiled Spirit to the created soul, so that it grows as it ought and sees what it should.

Thy heavens (some say,)
Are a firy-liquid light,
Which mingling aye,
Streames, and flames thus to the sight.
Come then, my god!
Shine on this blood,
And water in one beam;
And thou shalt see,
Kindled by thee,
Both liquors burne and stream.

O what bright quickness,
Active brightness,
And celestial flows,
Will follow after,
On that water
Which thy Spirit blows!
('Midnight')

'Ezekiel's Vision' by Tanja Butler.

JOHN FREEMAN

Being There

Reciting to myself again those lines
of Rilke's, relishing the guttural
ach! and prolonging it *ad lib*, I think,
if sometimes I've been tongue-tied in the presence
of a higher, more composed intelligence
than my own, how much the more completely
would I be vaporised if an angel
were suddenly to take me to its heart.
I stop short at the end of the sentence, *ich*
verginge von seinem stärkeren Dasein,
I would perish from its stronger existence.
As my OTT rendering of it
echoes between the bedroom and the bathroom,
the last word resonates in my consciousness
like an *Om,* and suddenly I notice
as if for the first time, though I cannot
really have never had this thought before,
that in German the word for existence
is not just *Sein* but *Dasein*, being *there,*
with all the freight from the Upanishads
Da has, suddenly now reconnected
with the 'give, sympathise, control' of 'What
The Thunder Said' in Eliot's *Waste Land,*
an everyday Teutonic word disclosing
its identity as holy syllable,
and Being shown to be inseparable
from a place in which to be. Space and time
they tell us, came into existence
simultaneously with the universe
at the Big Bang, and they also tell us
not to mind not understanding this, neither
do they, but I do suddenly understand,
saying *Da-sein*, hearing it echo again,
how it would be like a flash of lightning

before I was annihilated to have
an angel with its overwhelming Being
there, or here, where I pause on the landing,
having been reading and writing all morning,
badly in need of a shower and shave. *Ach*
comes later, I always forget that. I love
its vehemence so much I say it early,
and can't regret it, it seems right, there
between the supposition, if an angel,
and the consequence. *Ach!* I would be toast.

RICKY RAY

Hunting for Good

All day he has walked
through the woods with his gun.

He has had the chance to kill.
Good chances, feathery, tufted.

He has raised his gun and lowered it,
leaving the bullets in their bed.

Now he takes his hands
to lesser killing in the garden.

Slaps his mind for thinking
leaflife somehow lesser.

At dinner his cat
jumps on the table.

Sniffs his plate, drops her tail,
droops and trots away.

As he retires to bed,
he looks out the window
and catches her
approaching a nest.

Bangs the glass,
scares her back,
yells her down,
but he knows.

She will crouch at the base of the tree.
She will wait for the reading lamp's dark.
She will slither up the bark in his sleep.

He'll wake to his body, then to his
knowledge, and question whether
a good man would put her down.

CHRISTOPHER MEREDITH

From a Sequence entitled 'Still Air'

Fumitory

The names are marvellous treachery:
mwg y ddaear
fumeterre
fumitory.
So what if they remember
some dead rite of burning,
some propitiatory cleansing?
Smoke is just a blur,
an ending.

No. Intricate fumitory is
a kind of opposite of smoke.
In these lines and frettings
mud weaves
tongues of petals that can sing
precision, counterpointing fractals
in a fugue of leaves,
condensing
earth to air,
to music.

Village birds

Villages are communities of birds as well as of people – William Condry

1

You landtrapped monsters
must be watched.

Sometimes you try with brutal energy
to rear into the third dimension

on heaps of stones
or with strange wings of fire.

The effort leaves you spent
your flat world waste.

We keep an eye and, most times, keep
a beat ahead

because you purblind
cousins of the worm

can't as we do see,
say, the quickness of a fish through water

or calculate the light's refraction,
can't feel through your oozy hides

the calms and freshes
of the liquid sky.

2

What blurry intimations we must seem
glimmering with the stars and moon

through the ocean over you
then sudden visitants

too quick in flashes of precision,
what was remote as dream

remade in meteor storms
of swifts' black syncopation.

3

We bring meaning
to your heapings of the curious rocks.

Those chimneys are evolved
for purging jackdaws' ticks.

The privet rooms are meant for us.
We hold our councils on your walls

notate on staves you draw with wires
polyphonies you'll never hear

and play their concert
in a hall of winds.

4

So you spread offerings for us,
your half-seen gods.

Sometimes, with bobbing circumspection,
we accept.

If we as you had words and gods
perhaps we'd worship you

as you also pray before
the creatures that you eat.

We might then, even, pity
bottom-dwellers crawling in mud roads.

But we don't.
We didn't ask your suffering

for us whose miles-deep parish is
the teeming air.

Ghost

And once in late summer,
the cool ridge grown dark
under bloodmarbled sundown,

from fern surge and gorse drift
its cries patching silence
came one low voice chiming

in still air and stirred air
conversing with absence
alone on a sapling

unmoving unceasing
and paler than frost smoke
the mistle ghost singing.

EITHNE LANNON

Pulse

I will lead you by the hand to the hushed hum
of the gentle oak, an evening breeze sounding

shivers into leaves, quiet turbulence in the air
and the gravity of sound settling on mossed stone.

I hear its tongue-lick in ivy the way a bat hears
the silhouette of trees, or a whale the shape of its home,

touching the skin like sound braille, tiny neck hairs
startled to its presence; earthmusic in the trees

and in the stony wind, atoms of light trembling in tiny
dust particles where body-bones separate, flesh disappears.

Between heart-pulse and light's shadow-touch,
I will lead you to the quiet abundance of silence,

the wide emptying of voiceless things; earth's pulse,
seamless and somewhere beyond absence.

Thin Places[1]

The wild meadow weave, the strand,
places of late summer, autumn.

A stone skimming water, suspended
in air, its slow-motion glide punctuated

by the drop, touch, rise of a ghostly presence,
this wary hesitation between water

and stone, mysterious as the rift between
music notes in air, unsettling the familiar light

which shudders again with tiny rainbow bubbles
holding air-drops in. And then the final slide over

gravity's edge, into polished bottomless depths,
beyond the belly-aching threshold,

dropping, ever dropping, into the quiet
whispering, the unspeakable tenderness.

---

1 The term 'Thin Places' comes from pre-Christian Celtic culture. It refers to places where the physical and non-physical worlds meet.

CAROL DEVAUGHN

Passing Through
for my brother

Evening

Light, having been itself all day,
couples with shadow, softens its gaze

and the forget-me-nots respond –
their quiet intense blue goes in, a little

as if rain had come and gone
without our knowing,

unweaving fibres, releasing the indelible.

*

Evening shadows know about longing –
the way they always lean towards,
never away from, intimation

the way they seem to give back
some of the light they've taken,
let it flourish for a while longer –

reflecting before being absorbed;

and finally the shadows themselves
losing the lingering moment
between revealing, concealing

as they are drawn deeper
and deeper in, like eyes opening
and closing for the last time.

Sunrise

Early morning, the day of your funeral,
you sit up, alert
the coffin – your launch pad.

You could fly, do anything now,
but you stay still, gaze straight ahead,
looking at something I cannot see,

focusing the way you always could –
seeing a thing in its entirety.
Perhaps you're watching your body burn,

especially your hands – flaming
like the pastels you loved to draw with –
watching them curl, melt into the driven day.

Midnight

The dark swells, loaded with half-hidden light –
you're going up the stone steps to the hillside,
leaving a trail of colour: burnt orange and lapis blue,
saffron yellow and deep mauve, as if sowing pairs,
a sower streaming his way, not in a field at sunset
but along a narrow passage at midnight to the dark
that swallows everything. You turn around, gaze
at me, disappear behind the pine tree we planted
on the edge of the woods. A sapling decades ago,
it became our giant gatekeeper to other worlds.
Now your way through is assured, and easier
without flesh and bones – on your journey you
might even fly over the wheatfields of Auvers,
and further on, land in a bonsai garden of stones.

Henry Vaughan's Ars Poetica

ROBERT WILCHER

I

When Henry Vaughan's poetry gradually emerged from the oblivion into which it had fallen during the eighteenth century, its rediscovery was largely in the hands of Anglican clergymen, from the Revd. John Mitford and the Revd. Richard Cattermole, who included some of his poems in their selections of sacred poetry in 1827 and 1835 respectively, to the Revd. H.F. Lyte, who edited the first complete collection of the devotional verses in 1847, and the Revd. Alexander B. Grosart, who edited the first complete works in 1871.[1] For these men and their readers, Vaughan was valued more for the devotional content of his poetry than for his artistic abilities. Even the poet Edmund Blunden, in the first book-length study of his poetry in 1927, regarded his verse 'as chiefly the intimate record of his spiritual life'.[2] It was no wonder that Frank Kermode caused such a stir in 1950, when he set about exposing what he saw as 'the critical error of refusing to treat Vaughan's poetry as poetry so long as it may be treated as prayer'.[3] E.C. Pettet, in 1960, was the first critic to attempt a wide-ranging analysis of the ingredients of Vaughan's poetic art—tracing allusions, identifying recurrent patterns of imagery, examining his sound-texture and manipulation of rhythm—but it was James Simmonds, in his 1971 book *Masques of God*, who provided a sustained demonstration that Vaughan was far from being the 'artless poet whose artlessness was a necessary condition of his distinctive

1 *Sacred Specimens, Selected from Early English Poets*, ed. by Revd. John Mitford (1827); *Sacred Poetry of the Seventeenth Century*, Vol. 2, ed. by Revd. Richard Cattermole (1835); *Silex Scintillans: Sacred Poems and Private Ejaculations by Henry Vaughan*, ed. by Revd. H.F. Lyte (London: Pickering, 1847); *The Works in Verse and Prose Complete of Henry Vaughan*, ed. by Revd. Alexander B. Grosart, 4 vols. 'The Fuller Worthies' Library' (Blackburn, 1871).

2 Edmund Blunden, *On the Poems of Henry Vaughan: Characteristics and Intimations* (London: Richard Cobden-Sanderson, 1927), p. 45.

3 Frank Kermode, 'The Private Imagery of Henry Vaughan', *Review of English Studies*, n.s. 1 (1950), p. 208.

achievement'.[4] The ensuing discussion of various aspects of his poetic craftsmanship called into question a critical vocabulary—dominated by such terms as 'nostalgia', 'yearning', 'ideal', 'visionary', 'otherworldly', and 'mystical'—that had yielded 'a composite portrait of Vaughan as a kind of simpleminded saint'.[5] Simmonds began his chapter on what Vaughan owed to the example of Ben Jonson for the development of his own craft by posing a number of fundamental questions:

> What were his poetic aims and standards of poetic excellence? What was his conception of poetry's nature and function and of his role as a poet? What did *Vaughan* think he was trying to do?[6]

Implicit and explicit answers to these questions can be found scattered throughout Vaughan's writings and the purpose of the present essay is to bring them together into an *ars poetica* that can be seen evolving over the ten years that saw the publication of his major volumes of poetry between 1646 and 1655.

II

What Vaughan thought 'he was trying to do' as a poet is bound up with the questions of what kind of poet he was striving to be and what kind of readership he had in mind; and the clues that can be picked up from his own published works reveal an ongoing transformation of his authorial persona and literary purpose in response to historical events that were transforming the world in which he wrote. That process turned '*Henry Vaughan*, Gent.' on the title-page of *Poems* (1646) into the 'Henry Vaughan, *Silurist*' blazoned on the title-pages of the two editions of *Silex Scintillans*, *Olor Iscanus*, *The Mount of Olives*, and *Flores Solitudinis* (the last two volumes being collections of original and translated prose) between 1650 and 1655. As Alan Rudrum has pointed out, both the abbreviation 'Gent.' and the title 'Mr.' affirm Vaughan's status as a member of the Welsh gentry and as equal in social class to the classically educated sons of the English 'hierarchy' that ruled Wales.[7] A claim to gentility and

4 E.C. Pettet, *Of Paradise and Light: A Study of Vaughan's Silex Scintillans* (Cambridge: Cambridge University Press, 1960); James D. Simmonds, *Masques of God: Form and Theme in the Poetry of Henry Vaughan* (Pittsburgh: University of Pittsburgh Press, 1972), p. 8.

5 Simmonds, *Masques of God*, pp. 7-8.

6 *Masques of God*, p. 23.

7 Alan Rudrum, 'Paradoxical Persona: Henry Vaughan's Self-Fashioning', *Huntington Library Quarterly*, 62 (1999), pp. 355-56.

cultivated taste is also made in the dedication of his first volume of poetry to the '*more refined* spirits' of the 'Ingenious Lovers of Poesy' who will know how to value his original 'fancies' and to appreciate his translation of Juvenal better than the dull 'spirits' of those who never '*soar above the drudgery of dirty* intelligence' and are ignorant of Latin.[8] A similar claim is made in the opening poem addressed to his 'Ingenuous Friend, *R.W.*', who shares 'one mind' with him and with 'the wiser few' aspires to join other 'learned ghosts' in honouring 'Great *BEN*' and his acolyte, Thomas Randolph, in 'the Elysian fields' of poetic immortality.[9] During the 1640s, the epithet 'ingenious' (sometimes spelt 'ingenuous') had gathered specifically elitist and often royalist connotations from its use to promote the poetic volumes of Edmund Waller (1645), John Milton (1645), and the archetypal Cavalier, Sir John Sucking' (1646).[10] Vaughan's 'A Rhapsody', which was 'occasionally written upon a meeting with some of his friends at the Globe Tavern', reflects the ethos of the gatherings that Jonson had earlier presided over in the Apollo Room at the St Dunstan and Devil Tavern near Temple Bar:

> Drink deep; this cup be pregnant; & the wine
> Spirit of wit, to make us all divine,
> That big with sack, and mirth we may retire
> Possessors of more souls, and nobler fire; . . .
> So, if a nap shall take us, we shall all,
> After full cups have dreams poetical.[11]

Simmonds observed that when Vaughan invoked 'an ultimate standard in poetry' during the 1640s, 'he spoke of Ben Jonson'; and looking further afield to poetic developments in the pre-war Caroline decade, Jonathan Post suggests that when Vaughan spoke of the '*fire*' of his amatory verse as 'but Platonic', he

8 *Henry Vaughan: The Complete Poems*, ed. by Alan Rudrum (Harmondsworth: Penguin Books, 1976; revised 1983), p. 31. Hereafter cited as *R*.

9 *R*, p. 32.

10 In his prefaces, Humphrey Moseley had recommended Waller's volume to 'gentle' readers, who appreciated 'the choycest sort of invention', and Suckling's *Fragmenta Aurea* to 'the Ingenuous Reader', while noting that Waller's *Poems* had been given a favourable reception by 'the most ingenious men' in his introduction to Milton. See John Curtis Reed, 'Humphrey Moseley, Publisher', *Proceedings and Papers of the Oxford Bibliographical Society*, 2 (1927-1930), pp. 76-77, 75.

11 *R*, pp. 40-42. For an account of proceedings in the Apollo Room, see Stella Achilleos, 'The *Anacreontea* and a Tradition of Refined Male Sociability', in *A Pleasing Sinne: Drink and Conviviality in Seventeenth-Century England*, ed. by Adam Smyth (Cambridge: D.S. Brewer, 2004), pp. 25-30.

was indicating 'his allegiance to some of the *précieuse* fashions of the day', typified by William Habington's *Castara* (1634, 1635, 1640).[12]

A second collection of secular verse had been prepared for the press by the end of 1647, but its publication was delayed until 1651. A prefatory letter by the 'publisher' revealed that the poet '*had long ago condemned these* poems *to* obscurity' and confessed that he did not have '*the author's* approbation *to the* fact' of making them public.[13] Evidently something had happened to change Vaughan's mind about the value of the poetry he had been writing up to the end of 1647, when he composed a dedication of the volume to Lord Kildare Digby.[14] Some of the poems originally intended for inclusion were replaced by occasional poems that date from the years 1648-1651, and it is widely agreed that the verse translations from Boethius and Casimire, along with the four prose translations, were not in the collection that had been made ready for the press in 1647.[15] The information on the title page that the 'Poems, and Translations' were 'Formerly written by *Mr.* Henry Vaughan *Silurist*' and were 'Published by a Friend' serves to distance the poet himself from the process of publication and has generated a good deal of debate.[16]

A possible scenario for the publication of *Olor Iscanus*, taking account of a gradual change in Vaughan's attitude towards the nature and purpose of poetry, has recently been adumbrated by Jonathan Nauman. He notes that the commendatory verses by Thomas Powell prefixed to *Thalia Rediviva* (1678)—some eighteen years after their author's death—must have been written originally to introduce what Powell called the '*Ingenious* Poems' in the aborted 1647 volume, which was clearly intended to be 'a Cavalier celebration of '*Love*' and '*War*''. In the event, the most prominent topics in *Olor Iscanus* were 'Royalist stoicism and disillusionment, literary appreciation, acceptance of retirement', so that the volume as published had become 'an emblematic testimony to the fact that

12 Simmonds, *Masques of God*, p. 23; Jonathan F.S. Post, *Henry Vaughan: The Unfolding Vision* (Princeton, N.J.: Princeton University Press, 1982), p. 8. The claim to a chaste 'flame' is made in the prefaces to Vaughan's *Poems* and Habington's *Castara*.

13 *R*, p. 67.

14 See *R*, p. 66. He dated the dedication '*Newton* by *Usk* this 17. of Decemb. 1647.'.

15 Some of the excised poems appeared much later in *Thalia Rediviva*; some may well have been completely suppressed.

16 In this debate, the following are among the most significant contributions: William R. Parker, 'Henry Vaughan and his Publishers', *The Library*, 4th series, 20 (1940), pp. 401-11; Harold R. Walley, 'The Strange Case of *Olor Iscanus*', *RES*, 18 (1942), pp. 27-37; E.L. Marilla, '"The Publisher to the Reader" of *Olor Iscanus*', *RES*, 24 (1948), pp. 36-41; F.E. Hutchinson, *Henry Vaughan: A Life and Interpretation* (Oxford: Clarendon Press, 1947), pp. 75-77; Alan Rudrum, 'Some Remarks on Henry Vaughan's Secular Poems', *Poetry Wales*, 11 (1975), pp. 45-46; Thomas Willard, '"The Publisher to the Reader" of *Olor Iscanus*', *Papers of the Bibliographical Society of America*, 75 (1981), pp. 174-77; Post, *The Unfolding Vision*, p. 27.

Vaughan's poetic energies had turned elsewhere'.[17] Indeed, the first edition of *Silex Scintillans* had appeared in 1650 before the altered collection of 1647 was issued in the middle of 1651.[18] Nauman's plausible explanation of the delay is that the process of publication by Humphrey Moseley was interrupted by Royalist uprisings in Wales and the death in July 1648 of Vaughan's younger brother, William, probably as a result of his participation. Vaughan would not have been, as Nauman puts it, 'of a mind to publish a defiant Cavalier celebration after the summer of 1648'.[19] By the time he emerged from a period of mourning, Henry had already experienced the beginnings of that change of heart and direction that would turn him into a poetic disciple of 'the blessed man, Mr. *George Herbert*'.[20] The 'friend', who acted as his agent in London (almost certainly his twin brother, Thomas), felt bound to honour the agreement he had made with Moseley and persuaded his reluctant twin to allow him to excise from the manuscript 'all poems merely on amatory or martial themes' and to supplement what was left with more recent occasional poems and translations that were not blatantly at odds with his new religious sensibilities.[21]

There are many indications in the poems themselves of the poetic tradition that Vaughan was anxious to align himself with during the initial phase of his literary career. For example, the first of the translations from Ovid's *Tristia*—among the earliest of the writings assembled in *Olor Iscanus*—is addressed to the 'blithe god of *sack*', the inspirational drink celebrated by Jonson and his followers; and later in the poem, the friends that the exiled Ovid had left behind in Rome become the more Jonsonian 'jolly crew / Of careless *poets*' whose metropolitan company the Welsh poet misses in his isolation in rural Breconshire. Vaughan is recalling the kind of '*Lyrick* Feasts' celebrated in Robert Herrick's ode for Ben Jonson, when the master's verse 'out-did the frolick wine', and in his own 'A Rhapsody', with its paean to 'royal, witty sack, the poets' soul'.[22] In

17 Jonathan Nauman, 'Toward a Herbertian Poetic: Vaughan's Rigorism and "The Publisher to the Reader" of *Olor Iscanus*', *George Herbert Journal*, 23 (1999), p. 93. Powell's claim that the poems are designed 'to charm our *Civil* Rage', when 'steeled *Mars*' and '*Love*' are rivals for the attention of '*Poesy*', suggests a volume that was predominantly in the Cavalier manner (*R*, p. 321).

18 *Silex Scintillans* was registered on 28 March 1650; *Olor Iscanus* was registered on 28 April 1651.

19 Nauman, 'Toward a Herbetian Poetic', 93.

20 *R*, p. 142.

21 Nauman, 'Toward a Herbertian Poetic', 95-100.

22 See *R*, pp. 99, 100, 40. Walley regards the translations from Ovid as 'unquestionably the earliest translations' ('The Strange Case of *Olor Iscanus*', 32). For Herrick's 'An Ode for him', see *The Complete Poetry of Robert Herrick*, ed. by Tom Cain and Ruth Connolly, 2 vols. (Oxford: Oxford University Press, 2013), I, p. 275. In an essay entitled 'Sons of Beer and Sons of Ben: Drink as a Social Marker in Seventeenth-Century England', Cedric Brown comments on Robert Herrick's 'The Welcome to Sack' that 'The refined drink is a kind of wine, and only wine supports the Muse. Both poetry and wine are signs of an exclusive society, and Sons of Beer can have no pretensions to refined understanding' (*A Pleasing Sinne*, p. 7).

the volume's opening poem, 'To the River Isca', his stated aspiration is to emulate Petrarch, Ausonius, Sidney, and Habington in imparting poetic immortality to his native stream; in 'Monsieur Gombauld', he praises the 'richer thoughts' and 'rare fancy' of the author of a prose romance, *Endymion* (1624), which had recently appeared in an English version; he greets the 1647 folio edition of the plays of Beaumont and Fletcher as a relief from the '*dearth* of wit' in contemporary literature and singles out John Fletcher as second only to Jonson in outdoing 'all *future wits*' and matching those of 'the *past*'; the commendatory verses printed along with many others in the posthumous collection of William Cartwright's poems and plays maintain that '*wit*' was 'at her *zenith*' in his work, where 'not a *line* (to the most *critic* he) / Offends with *flashes*, or *obscurity*'; and the 'witty fair one', Katherine Philips, is complimented not only for her 'rich numbers' but also for avoiding 'coarse trifles' and 'matter borrow'd from the age'.[23] Though approving of 'wit' and 'fancy', Vaughan values Jonsonian perspicuity above the '*flashes*, or *obscurity*' of the far-fetched conceits and arcane arguments associated with Donne and his disciples. The latest of the original items added to the volume, however, contains none of the emphasis on wit and technical skill in the other literary tributes but focusses instead on the chasteness with which the love affairs in William Davenant's *Gondibert* are depicted, so that 'their *language*, and their *love*'—'Calm as *Rose-leaves*, and cool as *virgin-snow*'—'both *delight*, and *dignify* the mind'.[24] Nauman sees this as evidence that by early 1651, when Davenant's epic was published, Vaughan had already 'shifted away' from his previous 'ambitious and professional literary focus' toward 'an intensified appreciation of good poetry as an embodiment of a poet's worthwhile experience', which would lead to the 'Herbertian rigorism' of his 'scrupulous inclination to write sacred verse only'.[25]

III

Vaughan's eventual repudiation of social and professional aspects of the Jonsonian tradition was foreshadowed in the way *Silex Scintillans* was presented to the public in 1650. The usual introductory matter that mediates between the author and the world is missing: no preface, no epistle to the reader, no commendatory verses. Instead, there is an emblematic title-page accompanied by an explanatory poem in Latin—two of the elements in the 'tripartite, visual-verbal art form' of the emblem described by Karl Höltgen, namely 'the pictura

23 See *R*, pp. 70, 80, 87-88, 89, 95.

24 *R*, p. 98.

25 Nauman, 'Toward a Herbertian Poetic', pp. 85-86, 80.

or icon' and the 'explanatory Epigram'. The third element—'the motto or lemma'—is supplied by the title of the volume, *Silex Scintillans* (the flashing flint). Books of emblems were popular across Europe in the sixteenth and seventeenth centuries and some two hundred emblematic title-pages were produced in England alone between 1570 and 1660.[26] The Latin verses facing the title-page of Vaughan's 1650 collection make it clear that this is a specialized kind of emblem: *Authoris (de se) Emblema* ('The Author's Emblem about Himself') —a personal emblem, like John Donne's emblematic seal of Christ crucified upon an Anchor, which is explained in the accompanying epigram that the poet sent to George Herbert and other friends:

> *Crosses grow Anchors, bear as thou shouldst do*
> *Thy Cross, and that Cross grows an Anchor too.*
> *But he that makes our Crosses Anchors thus,*
> *Is* Christ, *who there is crucified for us.*[27]

Höltgen identifies the two main motifs of the personal emblem devised for *Silex Scintillans*—the arm reaching from the sky and the heart of stone—as common features of classical, biblical, and later Christian tradition.[28] Vaughan's emblem, however, is *more* personal than Donne's, which represents in visual form a universal message about salvation through suffering made available to 'us' through Christ's cross. In his explanatory poem, Vaughan addresses God rather than other Christians, relating in the first person singular the dealings of his Maker and Saviour with his own recalcitrant heart:

> You have attempted many times, I admit, to capture me without injury, and your voice, haunting me, has endeavoured without words to make me heedful . . . I was a flint — deaf and silent . . . You allow for my reformation by another means, and alter your approach; and now, angered, you deny that love can prevail, and prepare to overcome force with force. You draw nearer and break that mass which is my rocky heart, and that which was formerly stone is now made flesh. See how it is torn, its

26 Karl Josef Höltgen, 'Henry Vaughan's *Silex Scintillans*: Emblematic Tradition and Meaning', Reprinted from *Emblematica: An Interdisciplinary Journal for Emblem Studies* (AMS Press, Inc., 1989), pp. 273-74.

27 The seal and the verses are reproduced as Figure 2 by Höltgen, who notes that George Wither, Erasmus, Luther, Montaigne, Sidney, Chapman, and Quarles all had personal emblems or imprese. See 'Henry Vaughan's *Silex Scintillans*', p. 275.

28 Höltgen calls the heart-shaped flint struck by a bolt from heaven 'a narrative emblem, the emblematic narrative of a conversion, a record of affliction and spiritual regeneration' (275).

> fragments at last setting your heavens alight, and tears from the flint staining my cheeks . . . How wonderful is your might! By dying I live again, and amidst the wreck of my worldly resources, I am now more rich.[29]

The words on the title-page, engraved beneath the *pictura*, also emphasize that the collection contains both 'Sacred Poems' of a devotional kind and others that belong to the more obviously personal category of 'Private Ejaculations'.[30]

One other feature on the title-page marks a significant change of perspective: the persona of 'Silurist', adopted here for the first time, signals the abandonment of Vaughan's bid for recognition by the 'ingenious' cultural elite he had encountered in Oxford and London and a commitment to his native place, which had once been the territory of the Silures mentioned by Tacitus. Hutchinson interpreted the new title as merely a mark of 'his love of that part of South-east Wales', while others have detected a more political thrust in this allusion to a tribe famous for its stubborn resistance to invading Romans and Normans.[31] In Rudrum's view, the death of 'a range of hopes and aspirations' as a result of the upheavals in the state and in Vaughan's personal life meant that poetry, for him, 'was no longer a way of making a claim upon the world and what the world could offer: it fell back upon that function it had of old among the Welsh, of asserting undefeatedness in the midst of defeat'.[32]

Vaughan distances himself further from the Jonsonian affiliation of his secular verse by dedicating this new volume not to a patron, who might secure its favourable reception in the world, but to Christ, who is not only the recipient but also the originator of what the poet humbly presents to him as 'thy deaths first fruits':

> Some drops of thy all-quickening blood
> Fell on my heart; those made it bud
> And put forth thus, though Lord, before
> The ground was cursed, and void of store.[33]

29 *R*, pp. 137-38.

30 Vaughan may be primarily indicating his allegiance to Herbert by adopting this subtitle from *The Temple*, but the experiences embodied in many of these present tense ejaculatory poems—the untitled elegies, for example—feel more raw with conflict and grief than Herbert's past tense reports of conflicts resolved.

31 See Hutchinson, *Henry Vaughan*, p. 78; Eluned Brown, 'Henry Vaughan's Biblical Landscape', *Essays and Studies*, n.s. 30 (1977), p. 51; Roland Mathias, 'The Silurist Re-examined', *Scintilla*, no. 2 (1998), pp. 69-72.

32 Rudrum, 'Paradoxical Persona', p. 358.

33 *R*, p. 145.

In this new phase of his development, it is the blood shed by Christ on the Cross, rather than 'royal, witty sack', that gives poetic utterance to a heart that would otherwise be barren. Not many pages into the collection, there is a counterpart to the poem which opens *Olor Iscanus* by staking Vaughan's claim to a place in the long line of river poets stretching back from Habington and Sidney to Ausonius and Petrarch. 'Mount of Olives (I)', however, invokes the 'learned swains' who have celebrated '*Cotswold*, and *Cooper's*' with their 'pipes, and wit' not from a desire to emulate them but in order to disparage the 'ill-placed wit, / Conceit, or call it what you please' that has been expended in idolizing 'some shade, or grove', while the 'sacred hill' upon which Christ 'wept once' and 'walked whole nights' has been neglected by the poetic tradition.[34] About halfway through the volume, the imagery of the dedication is taken up in 'Unprofitableness' to express a more personal sense of failure to respond poetically to the 'all-quickening' presence of Christ, even though his 'visits' have revived the 'bleak leaves' and 'sad decays' of the poet's spiritual life:

> But, ah, my God! what fruit hast thou of this?
> What one poor leaf did ever I yet fall
> To wait upon thy wreath?[35]

The role of the heart in producing the kind of verse Vaughan now feels called upon to write is explored in 'Disorder and Frailty', which describes how God first took possession of it by beckoning his 'brutish soul' out of the 'womb of darkness' and how he still tends to 'pine, and shrink' and 'creep' into 'the old silence' when 'tossed / By winds, and bit with frost'. Like the 'gallant flower' in one of the elegies, he retires beneath the soil during winter, but he can break from his 'cell / Of clay, and frailty' and 'bud' again when touched by the 'fire, and breath' of God. That Vaughan is speaking about his practice as a poet as well as his experience as a sinful human being becomes clear in the final stanza, in which he pleads for 'wings' to 'fly' and prays that the 'seed' sown in him may not be killed by 'perverse, / And foolish thoughts':

---

34 *R*, p. 167. Vaughan refers to 'Cooper's Hill' by Sir John Denham and the poems by Jonson, Randolph, and others collected in *Annalia Dubrensia*, published in 1636 to celebrate the annual Cotswold Olympics that took place on Dover's Hill under the auspices of Sir Robert Dover.

35 *R*, p. 198. The life cycle of plants is one of the three 'major metaphors' for the spiritual life identified by Pettet in his study of *Silex Scintillans* and R.A. Durr devotes the better part of a chapter to exploring its ramifications (*On the Mystical Poetry of Henry Vaughan* [Cambridge: Cambridge University Press, 1962], pp. 31-60). The specialized use of this imagery to question 'what it means not just to be a Christian, but to be a Christian poet' has been more thoroughly investigated by Glyn Pursglove in 'Not with *leaf* only, but with some *fruit* also', *Scintilla*, No. 12 (2008), p. 35. He discusses the image in 'Unprofitablenes' at some length, including its connection with Herbert's 'The Flower' and 'A Wreath' (41-47).

But dress, and water with thy grace
Together with the seed, the place;
And for his sake
Who died to stake
His life for mine, tune to thy will
My heart, my verse.[36]

This poem is followed immediately by Vaughan's most explicit rejection in the 1650 volume of the kind of poetry he used to write. Entitled 'Idle Verse', it begins:

Go, go, quaint folies, sugared sin,
Shadow no more my door;
I will no longer cobwebs spin,
I'm too much on the score.

Such amatory verses 'gild rank poison, and allow / Vice in a fairer name'; they dress up 'Lust in robes of love' and amount to no more than the 'idle talk of feverish souls / Sick with a scarf, or glove'. He admits that his 'warmer days / Simpered, and shined' on such exercises of 'youthful blood'. But now that 'Winter is all my year'—in the dark days of mourning for a lost brother, an outlawed church, and a defeated kingdom—he is no longer interested in spinning cobwebs with idle words.[37]

A second poem with the title 'Mount of Olives' expresses the poet's joy when all his 'powers'—'soul', 'heart', 'blood', 'mind'—are animated by the presence of God felt variously as 'light' and 'breath' and 'balm', so that the 'cold thoughts' of a metaphorical 'winter' are blessed with 'a lively sense of spring'. The closing lines confirm the promise of the title that the underlying subject is once more the poet's dependence upon the Creator for the gift of sacred song:

Thus fed by thee, who dost all beings nourish,
My withered leaves again look green and flourish,
I shine and shelter underneath thy wing
Where sick with love I strive thy name to sing,
Thy glorious name! which grant I may so do
That these may be thy *Praise*, and my *Joy* too.[38]

36 *R*, pp. 202-04 .

37 *R*, p. 204.

38 *R*, pp. 238-39. In line with imagery in other poems on this theme, 'these' in the last line refers to the 'withered leaves' or pages of poetry that can be revitalized by divine inspiration.

The final poem of the 1650 volume returns to the imagery of the emblematic title-page and begs the 'King of Mercy, King of Love' to wipe out the 'shame, and sin' from 'the sullied, sinful book' of his life, since only divine artistry can 'reduce a stubborn heart'. As Donald Dickson has pointed out, 'Vaughan's metaphor links the flinty heart . . . with St. Paul's understanding of the new covenant, "written . . . not in tables of stone, but in fleshy tables of the heart" (2 Cor. 3:3 AV)'.[39] But the poem goes beyond this to affirm that only Christ's art of Mercy and Love, not the flawed art in the 'sullied . . . book' of a sinful poet, can achieve the 'victory' that produces those 'death's fruits' that were offered back to Christ in the dedication.[40]

IV

In most copies of the augmented edition of *Silex Scintillans* issued in 1655, the emblem and its explanatory verses have been replaced by a printed title-page and the volume is introduced by a lengthy preface, a page of scriptural verses, an extended dedication to Christ and the Virgin Mary, and a short untitled poem that begins 'Vain wits and eyes'.[41] The new title-page contains a motto from the Book of Job which gives the Author of all Creation the credit for the songs and wise lessons that follow—that is, both the aesthetic and the didactic dimensions of Vaughan's new venture into print:

> *Where is God my Maker, who giveth Songs in the night? Who teacheth us more then the beasts of the earth, and maketh us wiser then the fowls of heaven?*[42]

Although the formula 'Sacred Poems and Private Ejaculations' is retained on the title-page, another term makes an appearance in 'The Authors Preface to

39 Donald R. Dickson, 'Agency in Vaughan's Sacred Poetry: Creative Acts or Divine Gifts', *Connotations*, 9 (1999/2000), p. 179.

40 'Begging', *R*, pp. 242-43.

41 Jonathan Nauman has shown that there was some variation in the way in which the new prefatory material was incorporated into the second edition: most extant copies replace the 1650 engraved title-page, the explanatory Latin poem, and the short version of the dedication with the printed title-page, biblical verses, Preface, expanded dedication, and 'Vain wits and eyes'. In two copies, however, the printed title-page replaces the engraved one, but the Latin poem and short dedication are retained and the 1655 prefatory material is bound in the centre of the volume between the two collections of poetry. See 'Varying Arrangements: Observations on Some Copies of Henry Vaughan's *Silex Scintillans* (1655)', *Scintilla*, No. 20 (2017), pp. 9-17.

42 The title-page is reproduced in *The Works of Henry Vaughan*, ed. by L.C. Martin, 2nd edn. (Oxford: Clarendon Press, 1957), p. 387.

voice of thanksgiving'; the two stanzas added to the dedication in 1655 express gratitude to his 'dear Redeemer' for pardoning 'every published vanity' and confirm his belief that genuine religious poems are the 'fruits' of Christ's 'all-quickening blood':

> Dear Lord, 'tis finished! and now he
> That copied it, presents it thee.
> 'Twas thine first, and to thee returns,
> From thee it shined, though here it burns;
> If the Sun rise on rocks, is't right,
> To call it their inherent light?
> No, nor can I say, this is mine,
> For, dearest Jesus, 'tis all thine.

And the short admonitory poem adjures 'Vain wits and eyes' to submit to the 'holy fire' that purges and shed the tears that 'cleanse and supple', so that when illumination is granted—'Then comes the light!'—they will be ready and able to 'Praise him, who dealt his gifts so free / In tears to you, in fire to me'.[54]

In communicating his 'poor *talent* to the *Church*' towards the end of the preface, Vaughan places his book under the protection of Christ —'her *glorious Head*'—in the hope that he will 'make it as useful now in the *public*, as it hath been to me in *private*'.[55] Madeleine Forey sees this as Vaughan's announcement that the augmented edition of *Silex Scintillans* 'performed a substantially different function from the first edition'. Whereas the poems published in 1650 embodied the 'personal, spiritual' transformation of the writer—an essentially *private* response to the cataclysm of the late 1640s—'the new material of 1655 turned largely to the national responsibilities of the transformed poet, now prophet, within the context of the imminent general apocalypse'. In their new public role, the poems of Part One 'serve as part of a testimony of personal conversion', which gives authority to the 'prophetic voice' of Part Two.[56]

One of the central charges of the preface is against writers who not only 'study *lascivious fictions*' but also 'carefully record and publish them, that instead of *grace* and *life*, they *may minister sin and death* unto their readers'.[57] This

---

54 *R*, pp. 144, 145-46, 146-47.

55 *R*, p. 142. For the readership Vaughan might have expected in 1655, see Philip West, '*Silex Scintillans* and the "*public*"', *Scintilla*, no. 9 (2005), pp. 70-82.

56 Madeleine Forey, 'Poetry as Apocalypse: Henry Vaughan's *Silex Scintillans*', *The Seventeenth Century*, 11 (1996), pp. 174-75, 177. She compares this repackaging of the 'private' poems of 1650 as a 'public' testimony in 1655 to the self-authorizing methods of radical Puritan writers like William Erbery and Vavasor Powell (175-76).

57 *R*, p. 140.

theme is taken up early in Part Two of *Silex Scintillans* in 'Joy' and 'The Garland'. The first opens with a stern rejection of the sorrowful complaint, a poetic genre often associated with pastoral:

> Be dumb coarse measures, jar no more; to me
> There is no discord, but your harmony.
> False, juggling sounds; a groan well dressed, where care
> Moves in disguise, and sighs afflict the air:
> Sorrows in white; griefs tuned; a sugared dosis
> Of wormwood, and a deaths-head crowned with roses.

Though 'well-dressed', such self-pitying 'measures' are dismissed by the regenerate poet as a misuse of art, because the spells cast by these lulling 'numbers' distract from the life-giving inspiration to be drawn from the natural world and so lead to spiritual sloth:

> He weighs not your forced accents, who can have
> A lesson played him by a wind or wave.
> Such numbers tell their days, whose spirits be
> Lull'd by those charmers to a lethargy.

The true poet will 'ply' both 'eyes and breath' in contemplation of 'flowers', 'winds', and 'clouds' and will pass his 'solitary years' like a hermit 'in sighs and unseen tears'. Then, in place of the self-absorbed 'sorrows' and 'griefs' of pastoral complaint, he will bequeath to future readers a positive message about the spiritual benefits to be derived from suffering and affliction: 'And going hence, leave written on some tree, / *Sighs make joy sure, and shaking fastens thee.*'[58] 'The Garland' is addressed to a complacent purveyor of the 'willingly-studied and wilfully published vanities' deplored in the Preface:

> Thou, who dost flow and flourish here below,
> To whom a falling star and nine days glory,
> Or some frail beauty makes the bravest show,
> Hark, and make use of this ensuing story.

The personal parable that follows involves not only the pursuit of worldly 'pleasures' in his 'youthful, sinful age', but also his own poetic ambitions:

58 *R*, pp. 254-55. In the final couplet, Vaughan has in mind such pastoral works as Shakespeare's *As You Like It*, in which the love-sick Orlando vows to carve 'on every tree' expressions of his devotion to his beloved: 'O Rosalind, these trees shall be my books, / And in their barks my thoughts I'll character' (3.2.5-10).

I sought choice bowers, haunted the spring,
    Culled flowers and made me posies:
Gave my fond humours their full wing,
    And crowned my head with roses.[59]

This bid to become what Frances Malpezzi has dubbed 'a self-proclaimed *carpe diem* laureate' was brought to an abrupt end by an encounter with 'a dead man', probably George Herbert, which set him upon a different path.[60] The poem ends with advice on how to weave a garland of words that conveys life rather than death:

Flowers gathered in this world, die here; if thou
Wouldst have a wreath that fades not, let them grow,
And grow for thee; who spares them here, shall find
A Garland, where comes neither rain, nor wind.

Malpezzi's detailed analysis of the poem concludes that it 'directs itself to the role of the Christian and the Christian poet'.[61]

The contrast between false and true art is explored in a series of allusions to women from the Old Testament. The negative effects of the abuse of artistic talent are represented by Salome, whose 'soft arts' were employed to secure the beheading of John the Baptist, when she danced before King Herod. But Vaughan's chief criticism is directed at the man who first fitted 'loathed *motions* unto *sounds*' and invented the 'vain, sinful art' practised by the daughter of Herodias. Like 'wild *wit*' in poetry, his misused talents made 'grave *music* . . . Err in loose airs beyond her bounds', and like the vicious authors who are said to 'infect whole generations' in the preface, his corrupting influence outlives him: 'His *art* adds still (though he be dead,) / New fresh accounts of blood and lust.'[62] Already in one of the 1650 poems, Rebecca had figured as an example of 'sweet, divine simplicity', whose grace was beyond the art of 'a curled lock, or painted face'.[63] In 'The Ornament', Rachel's 'artless looks and dress' are a more explicit contrast to the 'latest modes of pride and lust' and the 'gay, alluring wear' that appeal to 'idle hearts and busy looks'; and in 'St. Mary Magdalen',

59 *R*, pp. 138, 255-56.

60 Frances M. Malpezzi, 'Dead Men and Living Words: Herbert and the Revenant in Vaughan's "The Garland"', *George Herbert Journal*, 15 (1992), 71. Malpezzi notes that William Vaughan and Christ have also been suggested as the 'dead man' (73).

61 Malpezzi, 'Dead Men and Living Words', p. 72.

62 See 'The Daughter of Herodias', *R*, p. 268.

63 See 'Isaac's Marriage', *R*, p. 161.

'*Mary's* art of tears' and 'art of love'—the 'cheap, mighty art' of the converted sinner—teach '*ladies*' how to make 'beauty lasting, fresh and pure'.[64] And finally, in 'Anguish', Vaughan appeals desperately to God for the same gift of repentance—'that art, / Which through the eyes pours out the heart'—so that he can get beyond a natural facility for versifying and emulate George Herbert in writing a '*true Hymn*':

> O! 'tis an easy thing
>   To write and sing;
> But to write true, unfeigned verse
> Is very hard! O God, disperse
> These weights, and give my spirit leave
> To act as well as to conceive!
>
> O my God, hear my cry;
>   Or let me die! – –[65]

Dickson sums up the Herbertian aesthetic that increasingly governed Vaughan's conception of the devotional poetry he was striving to write in the 1650s: 'To write the *true hymns* to which he aspired meant that his own part in their creation was secondary to God's'—only the 'indwelling presence' of the Holy Spirit 'will make it possible for the Christian poet to act and create'.[66]

Unlike those disciples of Herbert whom he dismissed for aiming 'more at *verse*, then *perfection*', Vaughan took upon himself the harder task of writing the 'true, unfeigned verse' that sprang only from the 'all-quickening blood' of his Redeemer. He would never have achieved his purpose of communicating his talent to 'the public' (and to posterity), however, if he had not possessed the poetic skills—first learned from the example of Ben Jonson—that enabled him to distil Mary Magdalen's art of 'tears' and 'love' into well-crafted sequences of words.

64 *R*, pp. 272-73, 274.

65 *R*, p. 294.

66 Dickson, 'Agency in Vaughan's Sacred Poetry', p. 182.

'Fruit' by Tanja Butler.

ROSIE JACKSON

Interrupted

i.m. Etty Hillesum, b. Holland 1914, d. Auschwitz 1943,
whose diaries were later published as 'An Interrupted Life'

In the garden centre, crammed trolleys carry
the weight of our longing for the perfect border:

Jasminum, Kolkwitzia, the yellow pompoms
of *Kerria*. Sunlight blinds us like a benediction

as I watch the woman next to me agonise
between *Helenium* and *Penstemon.*

How we take our freedom for granted.
Right now, if we lived elsewhere, we could be

holding our breath, hiding in cupboards,
our bodies eating themselves for breakfast.

Perhaps our mothers, too, planted daffodils
during the war, perhaps they buried hyacinths

in that very hour Etty Hillesum threw
her last postcard from a slow-shunting train,

registered light and shade as the dying
notice things, the sound of wood pigeons,

a final twitch of dark blades in that milky
absence we call sky. All our lives

are interrupted, we don't know when.
We take what we can. Give what we can.

Rabia and the Thief

Sufi mystic and poet Rabia of Basra (c. 717-801) was the first woman to become a Muslim saint

I imagine her here, in some quantum future,
her summers in hedgerows, winters in a corrugated shed
where she plays cards with God, who cheats, of course,

or plaits her hair, uncombed for centuries. She asks him
for a love that is out of this world and he replies
her soul is too old for trinkets. She does not lament

the garden of Eden, that sweet homeland between
the Tigris and Euphrates, once heavy with angels,
but prays for the whole earth to wake from pain,

to forgo its journeys to the black box of the Kaaba,
the crosses and synagogues, *asanas* of yoga,
all that greed for the honeyed sweetness of heaven.

Nor does she grieve at the loss of her beauty,
but welcomes the truth of what she will become,
lets herself be scoured by that longing for union

when she will take between her hands the much-loved
face on which the seven worlds are written, marry
that silence whose love leaves all words behind.

I think of her most when it's hot at night and I open
the window, remember the thief who climbed
over the sill into her sparse bedroom. Would I do

what she did? Recognise the smell of ocean,
know him as another creature out of water,
hair braided with kelp and badderlocks?

And, before he can snatch my blanket, fold
every piece of bedding, each last cotton sheet,
hand them to him like a dowry?

CHARLES WILKINSON

Forme

The breaking of its pages marks the end for a book
and who knows what's beyond words fixed in a forme.
Letters stored are 'all sorts' needing a hand to declare
a view. To make meaning, count on what varies;
understand that types are moveable, even when
the text coheres. Screw down the definitions and
remember how language, lying flat, must be pressed
in order to appear. Playing with verbs creates action
and existence; so then a series of ideas rises bright
as babies from new fonts: books so corvid-clever
you'd never think we would want for character
or plot, our clauses composed in crow-storms of ink.
Nearing the end-paper, yellow-skinned and foxed,
knowing nothing's left in the mould, each one of us
is a sole first edition. The glue's dry. Late years
prove what old binding lacks and plates fall out
as back and spine crack. The greatest fear cuts
an acid-burnt intaglio: what lies beyond gravure?
When all the words are broken will time survive?
If not, let's believe what we once thought and steal
back to the printers, to melt again and be re-set.

Forme: a body of type secured in a chase for printing

'all sorts': also an obsolete printing term – a collection of pieces of type representing letters or symbols

ALAN PAYNE

Mowing the Lawn

for Roger Hubank

When he mows, his mind lets go
of routes, equipment, descents,
the terrain of the fit,

but later, when he's coiling the lead,
he reflects on the ropes
his life depended on,

up in the mountains, with a friend,
an abseil from a perfect anchor
as satisfying as cut grass.

Hurricanoes

The morning after the storm,
I wheeled my brother-in-law
to the window of the library,
pointed to where a tree
had fallen in the car park,
talked about the wind
that had raged that night.

He seemed to understand.
It was difficult to be sure.
But when I quoted lines
from *King Lear*: *Blow, winds,*
and crack your cheeks!
Rage! Blow! You cataracts –
he broke into a rueful smile.

JOHN HAYNES

A Watching Still Awhile

for my son

A watching still awhile, a looking on,
a looking at, a looking through, as you run past
the cawing boughs, as if an almost Zen
applause is almost lifting from the grass
and through this see-through spirit which just then
I almost am, one of those ancestors
Maz* used to say he dreamt, watching again
what hadn't made his eyes turn wet before,
shaking his head, this witness still, this one
who's here, and so implied, implied of course,
no more than that, the constant that *I* happens
to, and looks out of, and has no source in

like a gaze under an empty hat,
seeing its soul so sprint away like that.

**Maz: Mazisi Kunene, South African poet.*

And then your Secondary School Ring Binder

for my son

And then your Secondary School ring binder
with its P2I, *Art, Detailed Scheme*
One brought my Year 2s back – open sketchbooks
first thing, drawings of onions on the walls
blown up like lines of fingerprints, or lines
of intertwining Bach, and quiet I never
had to ask for, like the field outside
where seagulls came down in long slurs
against first blue and then green with their wings
held still and eyes held still as they held fast
to having come so very far inland
from – was it? – home, to gently twinkling grass,

and quiet pencils, once my felt-tip's squerl
on the whiteboard, quite by chance miming their call.

SUSAN WALLACE

Timber

On a quilted shore washed almost clean
and buttoned down with shells, sand hot to foot,
we sight a timber, tar-black, ocean-rolled
to the smoothness of bone. Look: holed through here
for the hauling of ropes. There: see ghosts of whorls
that branched once and broke leaf. But after so long
a salting, its element is neither earth nor air.

So we hoist it shoulder high and wade it out
beyond wave-break. Ear to the grain, we hear it groan
in rhythm with the sullen heaving of pressed men harbouring
no hope of home; feel it tremble under the tread
of the fearsome Teach, flinch from the pyrotechnic fizzing
of his whiskers; or shudder at the splintering of round-shot
in some doomed pursuit of Spanish ducats.

The water welcomes it, lifts it, reminds it
how to swim. Here where Atlantic winds blow hard
it's far too deep for me. These days
I need to feel firm ground beneath my feet.
I fear the breaking wave, the world too wide.
Safe from the slow abrasions of the tide,
I choose now to be stranded, washed up, beached.

Henry Vaughan's Welsh Bird

SEAN H. McDOWELL

'For my owne part, I honour the truth where ever I find it, whether in an old, or a new Booke . . .'

Henry Vaughan, preface to Henry Nollius, *Hermetical Physick: Or, the right way to preserve, and to restore Health* (1655) [1]

As part of the scholarly recovery of the influence of Welsh culture on Vaughan's writings, especially those he wrote after his permanent relocation to Breconshire in 1642, we would do well to look more deeply into the rich Welsh poetic heritage. Some of the truths about poetic composition Vaughan appeared to 'honour' came from the 'old'—and even orally transmitted—'Booke' of Welsh poetry to which Matthew Herbert exposed the Vaughan twins during his tutelage. Indeed, the closer we look, the more we find, and what we find can help us resolve certain conundrums in the reception of Vaughan's poetry, especially both editions of *Silex Scintillans* (1650, 1655).

A case-in-point is the persistent criticism concerning what some perceive as the occasional architectural instability of some of Vaughan's verse, often focused on Vaughan's inexplicable variations of line lengths and stanza patterns. At several junctures throughout his critical history, Vaughan has been accused of structural lapses within his poems, even in *Silex Scintillans*. While most commentators acknowledge 'Regeneration', 'The World', 'I walkt the other day', 'They are all gone into the world of light!', and 'The Night' as accomplished masterpieces, other poems have not been favored with as much esteem. Often in such instances the fault is seen to lie in failing inspiration as a poem progresses. This was especially an early 20th Century criticism of Vaughan, even among erstwhile admirers. Edmund Blunden, for example, remarks of the otherwise 'striking' poem, 'The Stone', 'its effect dies away after a powerful opening, as so often

1 *The Works of Henry Vaughan*, ed. by L. C. Martin, 2nd edition (Oxford: Clarendon Press, 1957; rep.1963), 548. All of my quotations of Vaughan's prose outside of *Silex Scintillans*, including Vaughan's letters, come from this edition, hereafter cited as '*Works*.'

happens with Vaughan'.[2] For Elizabeth Holmes, 'Many of his poems, like the lines on "The Timber", begin with vivid inspiration, which later dies and leaves the rest of the poem dull and forlorn, because the gleam has returned to its source in the subconscious, and Vaughan's conscious mind, which is not strong or subtle, cannot follow it'.[3] Louis L. Martz cites the 1655 edition as a more common locus for such fading gleams than its 1651 predecessor: 'The common charges against Vaughan's poetry—that his poems often begin with a flash of powder, but then dwindle off into tedious rumination, that he works by fits and starts, that he cannot sustain a whole poem—these charges find their chief support in Book II of *Silex*, which reveals many signs of a failing inspiration'.[4] Even F. E. Hutchinson, who otherwise writes perceptively about the many influences on Vaughan's life and verse, is not immune from the tendency. In his chapter on *Silex Scintillans*, he delimits his range of inquiry by saying, 'for the purpose of assessing [Vaughan's] best work, we can disregard the merely imitative work of his immaturity and those poems in *Silex Scintillans* in which his inspiration flags or deserts him while he continues to moralize on a pedestrian plane'.[5] These and related perceptions of Vaughan's unevenness almost certainly account for why some of the poems in *Silex Scintillans* receive considerable attention, while others receive little or none at all. Yet such selective regard cannot help but result in what John R. Roberts twice said of Donne criticism: that by focusing on some poems to the exclusion of others it produces a synecdochical portrait of the poet, in which the part is taken for the whole.[6] Worse yet in Vaughan's case, one part might be made to indict others.

When a modern reader sees in a Vaughan poem a fall into mediocrity or a bright flame out after the first lines, the cause, in some cases, may well stem not from Vaughan's failings as a poet but from the way he tuned his poems to a different, more Welsh music than many of us are accustomed to hearing. 'The Bird', a poem from the second part of *Silex Scintillans*, offers a fit example. This understudied poem, a witness to Vaughan's recurring fascination with the symbolism of birds, informs Vaughan's perceptions of the overall significance

2 *On the Poems of Henry Vaughan: Characteristics and Intimations* (London: Richard Cobden-Sanderson, 1927), p. 28.

3 *Henry Vaughan and the Hermetic Philosophy* (New York: Russell & Russell, 1932; rep. 1967), p. 4.

4 *The Paradise Within: Studies in Vaughan, Traherne, and Milton* (New Haven and London: Yale University Press, 1964), p. 4.

5 *Henry Vaughan: A Life and Interpretation* (Oxford: Oxford University Press, 1947), pp. 165-66.

6 See Roberts, 'John Donne's Poetry: An Assessment of Modern Criticism,' *John Donne Journal* 1.1-2 (1982), pp. 55-67 and 'John Donne, Never Done: A Reassessment of Modern Criticism,' *John Donne Journal* 23 (2004), p. 1-24.

of earthly creatures in a meditative life. But more immediately to the point, it also exhibits some of the same stanzaic irregularities others have noted elsewhere. Here is the poem in full:

Hither thou com'st: the busy wind all night
Blew through thy lodging, where thy own warm wing
Thy pillow was. Many a sullen storm
(For which course man seems much the fitter born,)
Rained on thy bed
And harmless head.

And now as fresh and cheerful as the light
Thy little heart in early hymns doth sing
Unto that *Providence*, whose unseen arm
Curbed them, and clothed thee well and warm.
All things that be, praise him; and had
Their lesson taught them, when first made.

So hills and valleys into singing break,
And though poor stones have neither speech nor tongue,
While active winds and streams both run and speak,
Yet stones are deep in admiration.
Thus praise and prayer here beneath the sun
Make lesser mornings, when the great are done.

For each inclosèd spirit is a star
Enlightening his own little sphere,
Whose light, though fetched and borrowèd from far,
Both mornings makes, and evenings there.

But as these Birds of light make a land glad,
Chirping their solemn Matins on each tree:
So in the shades of night some dark fowls be,
Whose heavy notes make all that hear them, sad.

The turtle then in palm-trees mourns,
While owls and satyrs howl;
The pleasant land with brimstone turns
And all her streams grow foul.

Brightness and mirth, and love and faith, all fly,
Till the Day-spring breaks forth again from high.[7]

Architecturally, 'The Bird' challenges those who would approach it steeped in mainstream Stuart poetics. At 32 lines, it manages to avoid a consistent stanza structure. Each of its seven stanzas differs from all the others in some way, though stanzas one and two and stanzas four and six superficially appear to resemble each other. The first three stanzas measure six lines each and favor a ten-syllable line that scans intermittently iambic. But stanzas one and two indent their final couplets, and the final couplet of the former is composed of two four-syllable lines, half the length of its counterpart at the end of the latter. Meanwhile, stanzas four, five, and six are four lines each; but each relies on a different syllable pattern within its arrangement of four lines, and two of these stanzas indent alternate lines while one refrains from doing so. The fourth stanza alternates between longer nine- or ten-syllable lines and shorter eight-syllable lines; the fifth shifts to regular ten-syllable lines; and the sixth shifts again to a regularized alteration of eight- and six-syllable lines. The poem then concludes with a rhyming ten-syllable couplet, a return to the dominant measure of the line.

What are we to make of these irregularities? A closer look at the rich history of Welsh poetry suggests that at least some of Vaughan's stanza variances and other line-by-line stylistic effects can be explained as a conscious application of certain features of Welsh poetics, as expressed in the bardic tradition, to English versifying. Vaughan's Welsh-isms have been noticed before. Hutchinson, Alan Rudrum, Jonathan F. S. Post, Stevie Davies, and others have reasonably conjectured that both Henry and Thomas Vaughan studied Welsh poetry under the tutelage of Matthew Herbert, and that the bardic poets offered inspiration to the two brothers in various ways.[8] Henry's knowledge of, and interest in, the bardic tradition appears to have extended throughout his life. In his 7 July 1673 letter to his cousin John Aubrey, he lists 'A short account of the lives, manners & religion of the Brittish Druids and the Bards &c'. as among the books written by Thomas Powell, a phrasing that suggests a personal acquaintance with this book much in keeping with his friendship with Powell.[9] Another oft-quoted later

7 All of my quotations from *Silex Scintillans* come from *Henry Vaughan: The Complete Poems*, ed. Alan Rudrum (London: Penguin, 1975; rep. 1995), hereafter cited as '*Poems*.'

8 Hutchinson, 29; Rudrum, *Henry Vaughan: Writers of Wales* (Cardiff: University of Wales Press, 1981), p. 3. See also Jonathan F. S. Post, *Henry Vaughan: The Unfolding Vision* (Princeton, NJ: Princeton University Press, 1982), pp. 230-34; Stevie Davies, *Henry Vaughan* (Wales: Seren, 1995), pp. 57-58; and Sean H. McDowell, 'Herbert as *Bardd* in the Imagination of Henry Vaughan,' *George Herbert Journal* 34.1-2 (Fall 2010/Spring 2011), pp. 102-18.

9 *Works*, p. 690.

letter to Aubrey, dated 9 October 1694, shows a deep awareness not only of the ancient bardic tradition but also a personal acquaintance with then living bards still practicing their art. After a brief, nostalgic description of that 'very learned society' of ancient bards who neglected to put into writing any 'remains, or other monuments of their learning, or way of living', Vaughan provides a telling description of the 'later Bards' who lived right up until the then present time:

> As to the later Bards, who were no such men, butt had a societie & some rules & orders among themselves: & several sorts of measures & a kind of Lyric poetrie: wch are all sett down exactly In the learned John David Rhees, or Rhesus his welch, or British grammer: you shall have there (in the later end of his book) a most curious Account of them. This vein of poetrie they called Awen, which in their language signifies as much as Raptus, or a poetic furor; & (in truth) as many of them as I have conversed with are (as I may say) gifted or inspired with it.[10]

Vaughan subsequently amplifies his comments about bardic inspiration through a local anecdote later in the letter. Before turning to this anecdote, however, more commentary is needed on Vaughan's interesting choice of third person pronouns in the last sentence of the above quotation: 'This vein of poetrie they called Awen, which in their language signifies as much as Raptus, or a poetic furor; & (in truth) as many of them as I have conversed with are (as I may say) gifted or inspired with it'. Welsh was Vaughan's first language as well as that of his Brecknock neighbors, and so it was his as much as theirs. If Welsh poetic tradition was such a pressing influence for Vaughan in the late 1640s and early 1650s, one might ask, why distance himself from Welsh and the Welsh people through 'they' and 'their', as if to exclude himself from both when speaking to his cousin Aubrey?

We should use caution when weighting pronouns, especially when attempting to read between or behind an author's lines. In this case, though, the remark is so striking it invites exploration. Several mitigating explanations for Vaughan's choice of 'they' and 'their' (as opposed to 'we' and 'our') come to mind, beginning with the passage of time: between the publication of the first edition of *Silex Scintillans* and his remarks on 'Rhesus his welch, or British grammer', more than forty years had passed. The partisan pressures that initially drove Vaughan deeper into his Welsh heritage (i.e., the defeat and murder of the king, the dismantling of the Established Church, and the Puritan aggressions against Vaughan's friends and relatives) had diminished. Not only had both the

10 Ibid., p. 696.

monarchy and the Established Church long been restored, but also potential threats to the latter—for instance, Charles II's 1672 Declaration of Indulgences or the Catholicism of his brother James—had been neutralized. Vaughan in the years immediately before his death might well have been in a different place psychologically than his younger self, no longer unmoored, as that earlier self was, by the cataclysm of civil wars and Puritan victory and thus no longer as determined to so firmly separate himself from Englishness.

Furthermore, Vaughan's long career as a physician in Wales might well have introduced a new sense of separation between himself and the common people he treated. Throughout his life, Vaughan showed signs of a certain prickliness toward specific populations. Roland Mathias, citing a passage from 'A Rhapsody' (ll. 35-46), a poem he dates to the early 1640s, remarks, '[i]n this passage can be seen the countryman's dislike of crowds and the poet's very individual contempt for the populace and all its works'.[11] Decades of medical practice could have reinforced such an attitude toward common people but not necessarily toward his fellow compatriots as a whole.

For my part, the most compelling interpretation of Vaughan's use of the third-person pronouns stems from the apparent deep admiration for the bardic schools he voices earlier in the letter. Despite his tutelage under Matthew Herbert, whose sage instruction both he and his brother Thomas mutually admired, Vaughan did not undergo the extensive, nearly lifelong training associated with the old bardic schools.[12] Indeed, he could not have done so, even if he had wanted to. During the sixteenth and seventeenth centuries, the 'old tradition of Taliesin became more and more a matter of *vers de société*, lacking any significance wider than the events it commemorated'.[13] Yet even so, Welsh poets, descended from and trained in this tradition, still appear to have exercised their craft within Vaughan's hearing, and Vaughan admits to having both met and admired some. Given this admiration, the word 'they' might refer not to the Welsh generally but to these 'later Bards', and 'their language' might not refer to the Welsh language as a whole (which, again, belonged to Vaughan as well) but to the specific terminology with which these bards described their work and its intended qualities: 'Awen', the poetic term for inspiration, as understood within the bardic tradition.

Vaughan explains the bardic understanding of 'Awen' by way of the following story told to him by 'a very sober & knowing person (now dead)' about a young shepherd who one day fell asleep while tending his sheep:

11 'Reasons, Reasons,' *Scintilla* 4 (2000), p. 123.

12 See McDowell, pp. 105-06.

13 Tony Conran, *Welsh Verse* (Southampton: Poetry Wales Press, 1986), p. 66.

> there was a young lad father & motherless, & soe very poor that he was forced to beg; butt att last was taken vp by a rich man, that kept a great stock of sheep vpon the mountains not far from the place where I now dwell. who clothed him & sent him into the mountains to keep his sheep. There in Summer time following the sheep & looking to their lambs, he fell into a deep sleep; In wch he dreamt, that he saw a beautifull young man with a garland of green leafs vpon his head, & an hawk vpon his fist: with a quiver full of Arrows att his back, coming towards him (whistling several measures or tunes all the way) & att last lett the hawk fly at him [the young man], w^{ch} (he dreamt) gott into his mouth & inward parts, & suddenly awaked in a great fear & consternation: butt possessed with such a vein, or gift of poetrie, that he left the sheep & went about the Countrey, making songs vpon all occasions, and came to be the most famous Bard in all the Countrey in his time.[14]

Vaughan makes no commentary about this story after relating it; rather, stands alone, as if left to hover in the Marches between fact and fiction. Yet he precisely localizes it near his own home: the episode occurred 'not far from the place where I now dwell'. For Vaughan, the bardic tradition was very much alive, and nearby, even though the bardic schools themselves were in decline in the 17th Century.[15] We can see in his emphasis on 'poetic furor', perhaps, a glimpse of the kind of poetry to which he aspired in the visionary poems for which he is most famous. He seems to have known about such poetry, as well as the legends of the bards who crafted it, from his student days, if not earlier. It should not be surprising that such poetry gave him permission to explore his own visionary path.

---

14 *Works*, p. 696.

15 Idris Bell, in the translation of Thomas Parry's landmark history of Welsh literature, *Hanes Llenyddiaeth Gymraeg hyd 1900* (1944), describes the seventeenth century as 'the most fateful in the whole history of Welsh literature': 'As we look back at the period we can see today only age-old customs maintaining a creaky existence, with nobody who had any new vision or any idea at all how to escape from the old grooves. Not that there was any scarcity of poets—indeed, they were as numerous as ever—but that they lacked the learning or mental vigour to invent new methods or to conceive of any office for poetry except the social entertainment which had always been its function in Wales. It seems as if everything were running down to an end, slowly but surely, and nothing will remain hereafter but faltering echoes of the fashions followed by the masters of old, the work of the poet becoming less and less attractive to the well-born and educated, and more and more a medium of amusement or moralizing for the uninstructed mass; until the inevitable day arrives when no refinement of metre will any longer be possible, and even the language itself will have lost its brilliance and been corrupted by English words and vulgar dialect forms. A century of steady decay' (Thomas Parry, *A History of Welsh Literature*, trans. by Idris Bell [Oxford: Clarendon Press, 1955], p. 218). Conran phrases this decline in similar terms: 'During the sixteenth and seventeenth centuries, . . . the poets lost confidence in their own imaginative freedom' (66).

A close examination of his stanza structures and sound devices reveals an indebtedness to the Welsh poetic tradition deeper than simply the admiration for bardic inspiration Vaughan expresses in his 9 October 1694 letter to Aubrey. Welsh poetics seems to have informed specific features of Vaughan's line-by-line construction. As part of his broader reclaiming of his Welsh identity, Vaughan appears to have adopted a few recognizably Welsh attitudes and techniques, including his perceptions of the legality of stanzaic changes within poems. While two of the three families of traditional Welsh metres (the *awdl* and the *cywydd*) are fairly strict in their fidelity to a standard of line-by-line or couplet-by-couplet uniformity, a sequence of *englynion* may feature more than one stanza form, presumably for specific effects.[16] Furthermore, after the conquest of Wales by the English in the 13th Century, the *awdl* suffered 'a sea-change, becoming a two-movement symphony', in which a several *englynion*, often alternating 'kinds of *englyn*', would precede an '*awdl* proper' that was printed not as a block of text but in quatrains.[17] While none of the stanzas of 'The Bird' strictly conform to the conventional descriptions of the twenty-four traditional metres, several of them can be seen as free versions, lacking either the restriction of placing the rhyme on alternating stressed and unstressed syllables or the prescription of rhyming an end word with another syllable in the middle of the following line. Vaughan's preference here for the nine- or ten-syllable line here fits squarely within the *awdl* measure. But the larger point is that the Welsh tradition, through its encouragement of building stanzas from smaller units, could have given Vaughan permission to structure 'The Bird' the way he did.

This supposition is supported by Vaughan's unusual approach to rhyme in this poem. One of the four main types of *englynion*, the *englyn proest*, is characterized by what Tony Conran describes as 'a peculiar kind of rhyming (called *proest*) in which the final vowels must differ (though not in quantity) while the final consonant remains the same: for example, *den*, *ton*, *fin* and *ran* form *proest*-rhyme in English'.[18] Vaughan clearly opts for *proest*-rhyme in many places throughout this poem, most notably in stanza four, his turn to one of his favorite images, the star as a metaphor for the spirit:

> For each inclosèd spirit is a st**ar**
> Enlightening his own little sph**ere**,
> Whose light, though fetched and borrowèd from f**ar**,
> Both mornings makes, and evenings th**ere**. (19-22, my emphasis)

16 Conran, p. 323.
17 Ibid., p. 314.
18 Ibid., p. 320.

Strictly speaking, one could scan this stanza in isolation as a b a b (or g h g h in the context of the rest of the poem), in that the vowels in the first and third lines differ slightly from those in the second and fourth lines; but the stanza also operates as a single *proest*-rhyme, a a a a (g g g g), in that the consonant 'r' remains the same. Vaughan's choice of *proest*-rhyme here unifies the stanza —and by extension, the spirit-star comparison—more strongly than a more obviously alternating rhyme would.

A similar phenomenon unifies the first two stanzas. Earlier, I noted the superficial typographical resemblance of these two stanzas before also noting the syllable variations in their respective final couplets. The two stanzas are clearly meant to accompany each other as a two-part description of, first, the 'sullen storm' that 'Rained on' the bird's 'bed/And harmless head' (3, 5-6), and second, the bird's emergence, 'fresh and cheerful as the light', to sing its praises of God (7). Both stanzas begin with the same two end-rhymes: night' and 'wing' in stanza one, 'light' and 'sing' in stanza two, suggestive of the close relationship between the two. But this rhyming parallelism continues in the following lines, as the end rhymes of lines 9 through 12, 'arm', 'warm', 'had', and 'made', *proest*-rhyme with their counterparts in stanza one: 'storm', 'born', 'bed', and 'head'. Vaughan closely maintains the consonantal parallels so that each of the two parts of the one section describing the bird *proest*-rhymes a b c c d d.

When Vaughan shifts his attention away from this single bird to ponder the wider phenomenon of early morning hymn-singing across the hills and valleys of Breconshire, he changes his stanza again, though this new six-line stanza with its ten-syllable lines continues the habit of *proest*-rhyme:

> So hills and valleys into singing br**eak**,
> And though poor stones have neither speech nor t**ongue**,
> While active winds and streams both run and sp**eak**,
> Yet stones are deep in admira**tion**.
> Thus praise and prayer here beneath the s**un**
> Make lesser mornings, when the great are d**one**. (13-18)

While Seventeenth-Century pronunciation made 'break' and 'speak' sound more closely alike than they do to modern English speakers, 'tongue' and 'admiration' are less easy bedfellows with 'Sun' and 'done', but only if you expect the pressure of the rhyme to fall mainly on the vowel sounds. That same expectation does not apply to *proest*-rhyme.

We have already seen how the fourth stanza, a new stanza for a new thought, creates its own *proest* cadence. Interestingly, the only time when Vaughan adopts true rhyming patterns is in the final movement (lines 23-32), when he contrasts all these denizens of morning, these birds of light so obviously associated with the soul, with the 'dark fowls' of night, 'Whose heavy notes make all that hear them, sad' (25-6). Here he rhymes 'glad' and 'sad', 'tree' and 'be', 'mourns' and 'turns', and 'howl' and 'foul'. It is as if the change in birds warrants a change in poetic principles. These birds of night play by a different, more obviously English set of rules than Vaughan's Welsh bird of morning song.

Vaughan's choice of referencing owls is significant, too, not only biblically but within the context of Welsh poetry as well. Rudrum in his edition correctly notes the intertextual connection of these lines with Isaiah xiii, 21: 'owls shall dwell there, and satyrs shall dance there'.[19] In addition, the contrast between the owl and other birds figures prominently in the punishment of Blodeuedd for her betrayal of her husband Lleu Llaw Gyffes near the end of the Fourth Branch of the *mabinogi*. Originally created out of flowers to become Lleu's husband, Blodeuedd conspires with her lover Gronw Pebr to murder her husband and take possession of his lands. The attempt transforms Lleu into an eagle, who flies away into the wild. Aggrieved by the disappearance of his nephew, the magically proficient Gwydion, son of Dôn, finds Lleu, lures him progressively down from a tree by reciting three *englynion*, restores him to his human form, and then punishes the treacherous Blodeuedd by transforming her into an owl. 'And all the birds will be hostile toward you', Gwydion tells her in a modern English translation.[20] 'And it shall be in their nature to strike you and molest you wherever they find you'. To avoid the hostility of all the other birds, she must never show her face in daylight for fear of reprisals. In the process, her name 'Blodeuedd' ('flowers') is transformed to 'Blodeuwedd' ('flower-face'), presumably a description of an owl's face.[21]

Glyn Pursglove rightly notes that for Vaughan, birds are both 'fact *and* symbol' and that while 'The Bird' can be seen to anticipate such 'distinctly modern poems as, say, Hardy's 'The Darkling Thrush'', 'in other respects, Vaughan's poem is deeply embedded in much older traditions of symbolism, especially as represented by the bestiaries'.[22] One of these older traditions is the old Welsh bardic literature. None other than Dafydd ap Gwilym, for example, composed well-known poems about 'The Song Thrush', 'The Mistle Thrush', 'The Seagull', 'The Skylark', 'The Magpie's Advice', and 'The Owl',[23] and the influence of his

19 *Poems*, p. 607.

20 Sioned Davies, trans., *The Mabinogion* (Oxford: Oxford University Press, 2007), p. 63.

21 Ibid., p. 244.

22 ''Winged and free': Henry Vaughan's Birds' in *Of Paradise and Light: Essays on Henry Vaughan and John Milton in Honor of Alan Rudrum*, ed. by Donald R. Dickson and Holly Faith Nelson (Newark: University of Delaware Press, 2004), p. 253.

23 Or in their original Welsh titles, '*Y ceilog serchog ei sôn*,' '*Y mae bob Mai difeioed*,' '*Yr wylan deg ar lanw dioer*,' '*Oriau hydr yr ehedydd*,' '*A mi'n glaf er mwyn gloywferch*,' and '*Truan i'r dylluan deg*,' respectively. All six of these poems can be found in *Selected Poems of Dafydd Ap Gwilym*, trans. by Rachel Bromwich (Harmondsworth, Middlesex, England: Penguin Books, 1985).

poetry on Vaughan's may well be stronger than has been often supposed, a subject for future research. At present, however, it is enough to notice and perhaps to truly hear how the soundscape of 'The Bird', those regular consonant sounds shaded by varying vowels, is not confined to this poem or even to Vaughan's other meditations on creatures. Indeed, the closer we look, the more we realize Vaughan accepted *proest*-rhyme as a viable approach to tagging verses. This acceptance, in turn, appears to have relaxed the strictness with which he viewed rhyming generally. To our ears centuries later, it places Vaughan somewhat at odds with some of his contemporaries. For example, Andrew Marvell, for whom rhyming or chiming was a strong habit of thought, preferred the clear notes of a rhyme so much that he seldom off-rhymes and occasionally pads lines with filler words to ensure the rhymes occur with metrical regularity.[24] By contrast, the poems in *Silex Scintillans* contain quite a few instances of off-rhyming terminal vowel sounds and straightforward *proest*-rhymes, even if these occur merely as local solutions to a line or stanza and are not part of a larger structural intention, as in 'The Bird'. Many poems contain localized instances of off-rhyme, which strike the modern ear more as faults, lapses in poetic inventiveness, rather than nods toward a venerable poetic practice.

Consider the first two stanzas of the Soul's second speech in 'Death. A Dialogue', for example. These play with sound in interesting ways through *proest*-rhyme:

> 'Tis so: but as thou sawest that **night**
> We travelled in, our first attempts
> Were dull, and blind, but custom **straight**
> Our fears, and falls brought to contempt,
>
> Then, when the ghastly *twelve* was **past**
> We breathed still for a blushing **East**,
> And bade the lazy Sun make **haste**,
> And on sure hopes, though long, did **feast**; (15-22, my emphasis)

In addition to the chiming of six of these eight lines, lines 16 and 18 ('attempts' and 'contempt') are also off-rhymes of each other. These quatrains were designed according to an alternating rhyme scheme. Yet lines 19-22 constitute one recurring off-rhyme, with 'past' and 'haste' off-rhyming with each other as well as with the regularly rhyming 'East' and 'feast'. Given the recurrence of '-st' sounds, all four lines chime with each other.

24 For more on Marvell's attitudes toward rhyme, see Nigel Smith, 'Andrew Marvell and Rhyme,' *Explorations in Renaissance Culture* 35.1 (Summer 2009), pp. 88-102.

In another instance, the third stanza of 'Regeneration', Vaughan off-rhymes end words to create a different sort of balancing interlocked rhyming pairs in the presentation of his scales metaphor:

So I sighed upwards still; at **last**
'Twixt steps, and **falls**,
I reached the pinnacle, where **placed**
I found a pair of **scales**,
I took them up and laid
In the one late pains,
The other smoke, and pleasures weighed
But proved the heavier grains; (17-24, my emphasis)[25]

With the pairings of 'last' and 'placed' and 'falls' and 'scales', Vaughan's vowel sounds shift from short to long yet the consonant stays the same. This pattern ties line 17 more closely with 18 and 19 more closely with 20 through the ensuing assonance, as if the grouping of interlocking pairs were to reinforce the ensuing description of scales.

In addition to instances of off-rhyme that reinforce the content of couplets or stanzas, *Silex Scintillans* contains numerous other *proest*-rhymes that seem to appear randomly. Several instances occur in 'Rules and Lessons', most notably in stanza 17, Vaughan's advice about the proper conduct during meals:

To *meals* when thou dost come, give him the praise
Whose *arm* supplied thee; take what may **suffice**,
And then be thankful; O admire his ways
Who fills the world's unemptied **granaries**!
A thankless feeder is a *thief*, his **feast**
A very *robbery*, and himself no ***guest***. (97-102)

Other examples occur in stanzas 5, 6, 9, 11, 12, 16, 21, and 22. Two couplets in 'The Lamp' similarly *proest*-rhyme without apparent significance beyond this subtle rhyme variation:

I **watch**
That hour, which must thy life, and mine **dispatch**; (7-8)

and

Only, one point escapes thee; that thy **oil**
Is still out with thy flame, and so both **fail**; (23-24).

25 In all the block quotations that follow, the words in bold are similarly my emphasis.

The words 'this' and 'access' are rhymed in 'The Shower (I)' (8-9); 'hand' and 'forewarned', in 'Thou that knowst for whom I mourn' (9, 11); 'stir' and 'far' in 'Come, come, what do I hear' (11, 13); 'feast' and 'nest' in 'Holy Scriptures' (1, 3); and 'blood, 'good', and 'God' in 'Church Service' (20-22). There are two instances in the third stanza of 'The Check':

> View thy fore-runners: creatures given to be
> Thy youth's **companions**,
> Take their leave, and die; birds, beasts, each tree
> All that have growth, or breath
> Have one large language, *Death*.
> O then play not! but strive to him, who **can**
> Make these sad shades pure **sun**,
> Turning their mists to beams, their damps to day,
> Whose power doth so excel
> As to make clay
> A spirit, and true glory dwell
> In dust, and **stones**. (25-36)

In addition, this poem also contains the *proest*-rhymes 'crush' and 'flesh' (9, 11) and 'voice' and 'days' (37, 39). There are two instances in 'The Agreement': 'fits' and 'writ' (26, 28) and 'remove' and 'above' (41, 42); three in 'Mount of Olives (I)': 'love' and 'grove' (3-4), 'wit' and 'neglect' (11-12), and 'well' and 'hill' (17-18); three in 'Religion': again, '*voice*' and 'days' (18, 20), 'course' and 'worse' (33, 35), and 'increase' and 'seize' (37, 39), in addition to the off-rhymed 'have' and 'waive' (21, 23); and two in 'The World': 'scowl' and 'soul' (19-20) and 'lives' and 'thieves' (34-35), as well as the off-rhymed 'abode' and 'God' (53-54). All of these instances seem haphazard. Yet their prevalence suggests Vaughan accepted as normative a wider range of permissible rhymes than his near contemporary Marvell, a range in keeping with the received practices of the Welsh poetic tradition. As a result, it would seem overly simplistic to dismiss Vaughan's *proest*-rhymes as merely the product of a laxity toward rhyme.

Furthermore, *proest*-rhyming figures prominently in the overall architecture of several poems in ways reminiscent of 'The Bird'. In 'Love and Discipline', Vaughan once again employs *proest*-rhyme to bind separate stanzas into a conceptual unit within the larger design of the poem as a whole. Though composed of six stanzas, the poem contains only three divisible parts:

> Since in a land not barren still
> (Because thou dost thy grace distil,)
> My lot is fall'n, blest be thy will!

And since these biting frosts but kill
Some tares in me which choke, or spill
That seed thou sow'st, blest be thy skill!

Blest be thy dew, and blest thy **frost**,
And happy I to be so **crossed**,
And cured by crosses at thy **cost**.

The dew doth cheer what is **distressed**,
The frosts ill weeds nip, and **molest**,
In both thou work'st unto the **best**.

Thus while thy several mercies plot,
And work on me now cold, now hot,
The work goes on, and slacketh not,

For as thy hand the weather steers,
So thrive I best, 'twixt joys, and tears,
And all the year have some green ears. (my emphasis)

The first part, stanzas one and two (lines 1-6), contains two conditional clauses, both beginning with 'since'. Their relation to one another is apparent both in their grammatical parallelism and in their sharing a single rhyme, '-ill'. Both contrast an image of infertility (barrenness and frost) with God's active involvement in the speaker's interior life, and both end with a blessing: 'blest be thy will' and 'blest be thy skill' (3, 6). The thought of blessings then turns to a two-stanza reflection on nourishing and nipping powers of 'dew' and 'frosts', respectively. From the standpoint of English poetics, these two middle stanzas would appear to rhyme b b b c c c; but all the terminal words in these six lines—'frost', 'crossed', 'cost', 'distressed', 'molest', and 'best—*proest*-rhyme with each other through the shared '-st' sound, thereby furthering through sonic repetition the conceptual fusing of these two stanzas into one unit—the same technique Vaughan follows in the opening two stanzas of 'The Bird'. From this perspective, the first two thirds of the poem rhyme a a a a a a b b b b b b. While the last two stanzas lack a similarly binding true or *proest*-rhyme thread, they are inherently unified with each other as two parts of a single sentence. Perhaps Vaughan did not see a need for a shared rhyme here because he did not have to overcome any terminal punctuation separating the stanzas the way he did previously.

In both 'The Bird' and 'Love and Discipline', Vaughan relies on the chiming consonants of *proest*-rhymes to create connections between parts that otherwise might seem not as strongly unified. In 'Man', he explores the disjunctive potential of off-rhymes, specifically, the off-centeredness of vowel variances between off-rhymed words, to suggest the interior instability of human beings. One might consider these broken *proest*-rhymes, *proest*-rhymes corrupted by mismatching vowel quantities. The poem begins by establishing the steadfast reliability of the natural world as a prelude to establishing a contrast with human life:

I

Weighing the steadfastness and state
Of some mean things which here below reside,
Where birds like watchful clocks the noiseless date
And intercourse of times divide,
Where bees at night get home and hive, and flowers
Early, as well as late,
Rise with the sun, and set in the same bowers; (1-7)

Here, the regularity and dependability of the actions of birds and bees, like the diurnal rhythms of day and night, are matched by the regularity of the a b a b c a c rhyme scheme. But as soon as the speaker enters and describes the marked contrasts of the natural and human worlds, the rhyming words sound off-notes:

2

I would (said I) my God would **give**
The staidness of these things to man! for these
To his divine appointments ever **cleave**,
And no new business breaks their peace;
The birds nor sow, nor reap, yet sup and dine,
The flowers without clothes **live**,
Yet *Solomon* was never dressed so fine.

3

Man hath still either toys, or **care**,
He hath no root, nor to one place is tied,
But ever restless and **irregular**
About this earth doth run and ride,
He knows he hath a home, but scarce knows where,
He says it is so **far**
That he hath quite forgot how to go there.

4

He knocks at all doors, strays and **roams**,
Nay hath not so much wit as some stones **have**
Which in the darkest nights point to their **homes**,
By some hid sense their Maker **gave**;
Man is the shuttle, to whose winding quest
And passage through these **looms**
God ordered motion, but ordained no rest. (8-28, my emphasis)

In all three of these stanzas, at least one word within each a-rhyme triplet sounds an off-note in such a way as to suggest 'Man' is not quite in-tune with the natural world of stanza one. In lines 10 and 12, Vaughan offers an extra off-note by pairing the same long vowel with a slightly varied consonant, 'these' and 'peace'. It is as if the speaker's first appearance in the poem is accompanied by a representation of the restlessness he describes. Thus, the 'care' of rootless 'Man' strikes an off-note with 'irregular' and 'far' and is bound sonically with the 'r' sounds associated with 'scarce know[ing] where' home is, much less 'how to go there' (15-21). His restless knocking on doors and constant motion find additional reinforcement in the yoking of 'roams', 'homes', and 'looms', a fit metaphor for this back and forth 'winding quest'. The last rhyme of the fourth stanza—the linking of 'rest' and 'quest'—reasserts true rhyme. The poem ends, then, with a sonic promise of order restored. While thematically 'Man' recalls both Herbert's 'The Star' and 'The Pulley', as Rudrum notes,[26] it pursues this theme through a Herbertian usage of a Welsh device.[27]

Most of the time, however, Vaughan stresses the linking power of the shared consonantal sounds, in a manner consistent with traditional Welsh practice. Earlier, when discussing 'Death. A Dialogue', I noted the quadruple off-rhyme of the fifth stanza, which ties more closely together the 'past', the sun's 'haste' toward rising in the 'East', and the 'feast' of humanity's hopes. The recurring '-st' sounds, all equidistant from each other, sound a regular, persistent note. Elsewhere, Vaughan employs this same technique, the insistent, regular chiming of *proest*-rhyme consonants, as a means of creating closure in a poem. The 20-line, five-stanza poem, 'The Daughter of Heroidias', follows the rhyme scheme, a b a b c d c d e f e f g h g h i j i j. But Vaughan creates a *proest*-rhyme across the rhyming alternating lines of each of his last two stanzas to set off the last movement of this poem from what precedes it:

26 *Poems*, p. 586.

27 In 'Tears' as well, Vaughan similarly includes off- and *proest*-rhymes in three out of four four-line stanzas—'*rest*' and 'least' (6, 8), 'have' and 'crave' (9, 11), and 'sin' and 'then' (13, 15)—to better convey a heightened, disordered emotional state.

But thou hast pleased so well, he [Herod] **swears**
And gratifies thy sin with **vows**:
His shameless lust in public **wears**,
And to thy soft arts strongly **bows**.

Skillful enchantress [Salome] and true **bred**!
Who out of evil can bring forth **good**?
Thy mother's nets in thee were **spread**,
She tempts to *incest*, thou to ***blood***. (13-20)

While the repeated terminal 's' and 'd' sounds lend a greater sense of cohesion to the respective summations of Herod and Salome, the regular sounding of the same notes also functions a little like a phrase repeated at the end of a musical composition, a sonic means of telling us the piece is winding down. A similar usage characterizes the end of 'The Obsequies', only this time Vaughan moves more gradually into the terminal note on which he chooses to end:

Besides, those kerchiefs sometimes shed
                To make me **brave**,
I cannot find, but where thy head
Was once laid for me in thy **grave**.
Thy grave! To which my thoughts shall **move**
Like bees in storms unto their **hive**,
That from the murdering world's false **love**
Thy death may keep my soul **alive**. (25-32)

Six terminal 'v' sounds in seven lines, the same note over and over until the poem concludes. Vaughan's concentration of repeated consonants recalls the tendency of several of the formal Welsh metres to repeat terminal consonants in just this concentrated way. For example, *cyhydedd naw ban* is a 'nine-syllable line, rhyming in couplets, and often continuing the same rhyme throughout an entire stanza'.[28] But even in cases where a strong concentration of terminal consonants was not prescribed, it was not uncommon for Welsh poets in the old tradition to impose it. Dafydd ap Gwilym, for example, occasionally

28 Rolfe Humphries, *Collected Poems of Rolfe Humphries* (Bloomington, IN: Indiana University Press, 1965), p. 229. Well-known as a translator of Latin verse, Humphries also worked with Welsh metres in his own original work. His collection, *Green Armor on Green Ground* (1956), contained English poems in all of the traditional Welsh metres, along with an appendix that defined each one for an English-speaking audience.

adopted mono-rhymes in some of his *cywyddau*,[29] as in the case of of *'Yr Haf'* ('Summer'):

> Gwae ni, hil eiddil **Addaf**,
> Fordwy rhad, fyrred yr **haf**.
> Rho Duw, gwir mai **dihiraf**,
> Rhag ei ddarfod, dyfod **haf**,
> A llednais wybr **ehwybraf**
> A llawen haul a'i lliw'n **haf**,
> Ac awyr erwyr **araf**,
> A'r byd yn hyfryd yn **haf**. (1-8)[30]

This poem continues for another 44 lines, each line ending with the monorhyme '-af'. As with the Romance languages, Welsh lends itself more easily to rhyme, which is likely one reason why the traditional Welsh and native free metres place such a premium on it, both through the repetition of rhymes and through the rhyming of end words with syllables within lines. In ending 'The Obsequies' with such a concentration of terminal 'v' sounds, Vaughan implicitly shows us his ear is attuned to this native music. Even the sound he chooses to repeat resonates: 'f' in Welsh is pronounced 'v' as in the English word 'love'.

As all of these examples suggest, Vaughan possessed a keen eye for linguistic detail and a deep sensitivity concerning verbal sounds, perhaps a keener eye and ear than we have sufficiently given him credit for. Like Herbert, he could reinforce the content of his poems through the manipulation of the poetic means by which he conveyed it. Some of these manipulations are subtle and recognizably Herbertian. For instance, in 'Disorder and Frailty', Vaughan introduces a flaw in the execution of his stanza pattern to reinforce a sense that something is off-

29 Rachel Bromwich translates the *cywydd*, the abbreviated form of *cywydd deuair hirion*, as a 'song' or 'poem of two long lines' (*Selected Poems of Dafydd Ap Gwilym*, trans. Rachel Bromwich [Harmondsworth, Middlesex: Penguin Books, 1985], xv). Conran defines it as follows: 'Each line has seven syllables, and if the first line ends on an accented syllable, the second must end on an unaccented one, and *vice versa*' (p. 322).

30 Bromwich translates this stanza as follows:

> Woe to us, Adam's feeble breed
> for Summer's shortness (surge of blessing);
> by God, it is in truth most odious
> that Summer comes [at all] since it must end—
> with gentle and unclouded sky,
> and joyful, summer-splendid sun,
> and still and tranquil firmament:
> delightful the whole world is in the Summer. (6)

kilter in his 'brutish soul' (3). Each stanza follows an intricate, asymmetrical rhyme scheme: a b a b c d d e e f f g g d c. In the first three stanzas, however, the 'c' rhyme, which is introduced in line five and supposed to be completed in line fifteen, misfires. In stanza one, 'hour' (5) and '*love*' (15) make for odd bedfellows. The same is true of 'grow' (20) and '*weed*' (30) in stanza two and of 'steps' (35) and '*Star*' (45) in stanza three. In fact, in all three cases, these pairs of words, spaced ten lines apart, appear to have nothing to do with each other, much like the broken 'link' ''Twixt thee, and me' (9-10) the speaker complains of in the opening stanza. They come across as isolates, non-participants in the rhyme scheme. As a result, the poem might seem out-of-tune to readers with sensitive ears, but these same readers might not know why without looking closely.

In the final stanza, however, as an impassioned Vaughan asks God to 'give wings to my fire,/And hatch my soul' (46-47), the 'c' rhyme is fulfilled:

> . . . hatch my soul, until it fly
> Up where thou art, amongst thy tire
> Of stars, above infirmity;
> Let not **perverse**,
> And foolish thoughts add to my bill
> Of forward sins, and kill
> That seed, which thou
> In me didst sow,
> But dress, and water with thy grace
> Together with the seed, the place;
> And for his sake
> Who died to stake
> His life for mine, tune to thy will
> My heart, my **verse**. (47-60)

By finally achieving the 'c' rhyme ('perverse'—'verse'), Vaughan effectively counters his 'perverse' thoughts with mending his 'verse', a word that is additionally balanced in that final line with his 'heart'. The execution is worthy of Herbert.

Yet Vaughan's range extends beyond Herbert, too. His attentiveness to sounds encompasses his Welsh appropriations in ways that can go unnoticed. These can be hard to discern, but the closer we look, the more we can see—and hear—them. Throughout the 1655 edition of *Silex Scintillans*, Vaughan prints twenty-one biblical quotations, either as postscripts or as epigraphs to his poems.[31] This number excludes his Psalm translations and the poems he wrote from cited biblical episodes. Of these twenty-one quotations, Vaughan printed twenty in prose. But the last one, which serves as a postscript to 'To the Holy Bible' and immediately precedes '*L'Envoy*', the last poem in the collection, appears as a *proest*-rhymed couplet:

> Luke ii 14
> *Glory be to God in the highest, and* ***on***
> *Earth peace, good will towards* ***men.***

Coincidence? The likelihood that this printing is mere chance decreases when we note that this couplet pattern, a ten-syllable line followed by a six-syllable line, conforms to the *toddaid byr*, one of the Welsh *awdl* measures. Vaughan has suspended the requirement that the main rhyme occur one to three syllables from the end of the first line and at the end of the second, most likely because this internal-to-end rhyme does not occur in his original, and he would not alter his source to fit. Instead, he appears to have seized on the fact that the 'on' and 'men' in the original text *proest*-rhyme naturally. All he needed to do was print the text in a proper Welsh measure and capitalize 'Earth'. Vaughan places an obviously Welsh marker near the end the second part of *Silex Scintillans* just as he did five years previously when he concluded the first edition with 'Begging (I)', a poem written in the *traethodl* metre, a free version of the *cywydd* popularized by Dafydd ap Gwilym.

Twenty years ago, in his discussion of Vaughan's treatment of the grove image in 'The Book', the late Peter W. Thomas reminded us of the many religious and cultural frames of reference Vaughan was able to call upon at a moment's notice: 'In restoring energetic meaning to the grove, recharging the languishing image with Celtic, Druidic, Biblical, Alchemical and Therapeutic significances, Vaughan assisted in the divine work of transformation which (in the final words of *Silex Scintillans*) 'turned our sad captivity'', Thomas explains. 'The poetry of that captivity and defeat was "turned" in his pages too, to something new'.[32] To argue for Vaughan's conscious internalization of an allowable Welsh rhyming

31 These quotations are, in order, Revelation i.5-7 (post.), Job x.21-22 (post.), Hebrews x.20 (epig.), Daniel xii.13 (post.), 1 Peter iv.7 (post.), Song of Solomon iv.12 (post.), Acts xvii.27-28 (post.), Genesis xxiv.63 (epig.), Mark xiii.35 (post.), Romans v.18 (post.), Matthew iii.11 (post.), Romans viii.23 (post.), Romans viii.19 (epig.), Hosea vi.4 (post.), Hebrews vi.13 (post.), John xiv.15 (post.), Revelation ii.17 (post.), Jude xxiv.25 (post.), Romans vi.7 (post.), Psalm Lxxiii.25 (post.), Revelation xix.9 (post.), and Luke ii.14 (post.).

32 'The Poisoned Grove,' *Scintilla* 1 (1998), p. 44.

practice, or for his conscientious adoption of certain other Welsh poetic principles, is not to argue against any other influence, classical or English included. Rather, it is simply to acknowledge another of the many layers of inspiration that helped Vaughan shape his individual voice. It is to see—and hear—Vaughan's poetry more completely.

'Kisses' by Tanja Butler.

PAUL MATTHEWS

For Now

I like this hut. I like the smell of its pine,
the knots in its cladding where the wild
could break loose if it wanted.

I like how my jacket hangs so casually
from the door handle. Even the kettle
I never use assumes a right to its corner.

And now the rain comes, begging to be
let in out of the wet. Here's the trumpet
that Livia gave me, and if the portrait

of me on the wall is not quite a likeness
my face will change to accommodate it.
Some of these shelves are for books,

some books are for holding the shelves up.
Tomorrow I must give Julian his hat back,
but for now I will sit here

and wait for what's waiting for me –
like supper, for instance. Like the night,
fence by fence, finding out my hiding place.

Here Now

Hold dead still
until some winged thing
comes to the birdbath.

You have scoured
winter out then filled it

clean enough to chart
the seventy wrinkles
in your face. Don't

lean too close, though –
you'll keep the sparrows
dithering in the hedge,

or last year's song
might clutter the inroad
to this lustral place.

Three score and ten
adds up to nothing.

As your breath grows quiet
the wren dives through you
into its own reflection.

This Moment

You and I can see the garden
through this rain streaked glass,

and though reluctant to venture out
we could ease open the casement

and let that virtue whereby flowers
are engendered fill our quietness.

We could, yes. And all the while
vast powers beyond our eyesight

would be burying lovers like us
under rubble they once called home.

We need a window wide as Zodiac
for any flowering this engenders.

Hearts are Trumps

for Shara and Francis

We are teaching
whist to our grandchildren
on a terrace above the sea.

Tricks and trumps.
They learn the terms quickly.
The one who leads first
is left of the dealer.

But try telling the wind
to follow suit. Its sudden
gusts off the bay snatch
kings from our fists.

Inscrutable shuffler, it flings
aces and queens
promiscuously into corners.

You will learn its bluffs
soon enough, children.
Our brief summer together
has proprieties not to be broken.

From Left to Right

I your dark handmaid know how
to shape letters. Nothing stirs yet,

except that my spelling troubles
the day a little. It's risky, for sure,

glancing sidelong into the sinister.
It might tangle your tongue:

What mystery is this tricked out
with slick thimbles and rings?

I wish you could read me.
I spin gold below stairs. I cradle

your hurt things hidden in corners.
If you prayed I'd pray alongside.

This riddle of mine is the mending
of loneliness. Hold the page steady.

JAMES PEAKE

The Hum

‘Those who maintain that to discover the cause of an omen is equivalent to destroying it do not realise that, in doing so, they regret not only the signs sent by the gods but also those produced by manmade instruments, such as the sound of cymbals, the light of torches or the shadow on a sun-dial, all of which are examples of things produced by virtue of causes, but also in order to serve as signs.’

Plutarch, *Morals* (vol. 4)

1.1

It’s not white noise,
the crackle
of rainfall on an overwhelmed London,
acres of floodwater, the Royal parks and monuments,
the drowned volutes of car parks.

1.2

The Luxury Apartment

At this height
there’s more time, more daylight,

tiny balcony, fierce winds
and a lease

to the centre of the earth.

2.1

It's not white noise,
files and orts
ghosting through me,
painless as a time-lapsed brake light to the eye,
the glory and prose of passersby,
the nothing of either I feel.

2.2

The Would-be Venue

The ceiling's a mess,
burnt out circuit board of heat and soot
on bare cement,
running stains
from removed pipe,
a replanted smoke alarm.

Upstairs a muddle
of cheap furniture,

a three-legged chair
and sideboard,

bright wounds in its wood,
a piece of cutlery

in a keyless drawer.

3.1

It’s not white noise,
the rush hour burr
raised by a suitcase,
then a whistle, announcement
in an unknown language
and how an empty station
always arrives
at an equal silence.

3.2

The Club

Time is what things take
and a short set
of mirrored stairs
is enough to boundary
this world and another –

the club smells of cola,
sweet, and the shoeless dancer
dances to her own reflection,
slower in the glass
by a telltale fraction.

4.1

It's not white noise,
a shape inside which
voices cohere or change gender,
male to female, dead, living,
the mood like a legendary night
you left late but too early,
the thought of friends without you, the cold.

4.2

The Tunnel

The tunnel smells
of foreign detergent,

a warning-cleaning sign
scissored flat.

I emerge into a lack of starlight,
the fatty smoke from a stall.

An ex colleague
sits on the kerb nearby.

Hey.
She holds a shoe in two pieces.

Does she know or care
we were rumoured years ago?
The tops of her ears are cold.

5

The Open Window

A steady influx of ozone
and a clicking

like the airless
metal pieces

of a weapon,
the fallen rain

reassembling.

PATRICK DEELEY

The Ash Pit

What if a hot coal caused the dead
weeds, the nettles and husks
of Queen Anne's Lace, to spark up

and a flame to take hold
of the scabby pine tree that bowed
and scraped its existence from

the ash pit? This was, the men said –
humouring a child too full
of questions – what happened.

But what if the flame twisted
into a red squirrel climbing the trunk,
twitching as he fitted himself

between the branches? Shush now,
the men said, their hands
busy with implements and machines,

cleaving the timber in the long
loud sawmill. But she who emptied
the bucket of ashes, the bedpans

and eggshells, the stale crusts
from the bread bin and the tired skins
of eaten things, emptied them

every morning said let nature
sprout a new nettle, turn over a fresh
dock leaf, open the wings of

a peacock butterfly, start a sapling tree
out of a cone dropped
by the pine, said nature could allow

for its own design, fireball or squirrel,
fox, kangaroo, change even
the 'salt-and-pepper' Greenland geese

that grazed all winter in the Callows
into flaming flamingos if it
had a mind to. Imagine, just imagine.

Anthony of the Desert

Nowhere to whit my dull and lazy self, my boredom
down to size, but this wilderness of broiling sun
and sandstorm lash. I straighten to clarify
horizons shimmering mirage, bleached bones of camel
lying half-submerged a little distance uphill,

and in my slipshod sandals my bitten toes weep blood
as I trudge on – a stumblebum in the eyes
of the citizens of Crocodilopolis, worshippers
of the bejewelled reptile. Horned viper and scorpion
pester; primal devils threaten and tempt me

through the long dark's starry shiver. I find a tomb
to dwell in, drag the flat slab over, occlude
the world in tenacious dying while yet stirred to weave
prayer and palm leaf amid the saltbush beard
and dandruff of God. But soon again leprous limbs

come shambling and scraping; wretched faces
drip sweat, drip dusty mucus. 'You who know the soul
of nature,' they plead, 'tell us the nature
of the soul.' It doesn't matter how far I retreat
or into what stony hole. They close on me,

silly saint-seekers, discommoded emissaries of empire,
and those broken for whom I most hold love.
Readying – it doesn't feel odd – I drink the surly water
as God's given piss, eat the desiccated loaf
of misery he bakes, embrace his dune-drifting solitude.

T. Rex Skull, Ulster Museum

Dinosaur bones in glass cases, genuine articles
from the Antrim coast, lead us in
where this skull – no direct relation of theirs –

looms out of low light among the museum dead,
its huge snaggle-teeth grinning.
But whether God backtracked, or nature –

so full of funning – pooh-poohed,
or a chance meteor put the Cretaceous sunlight
and its children out, we find

illustrated here what the 'tyrant lizard' could do:
kill, devour, get rid. This sombre
convolution of bones – jawline, eye-socket, seat

of the brain – makes the ancient
ground-shaker 'exist' again, the legend appear
tangible and new. Yet even as a sense

of fellow-feeling outsits the awe engendered in us,
back of our throats a roar holds
ready to erupt, the threatened thing we can't

dismiss as vestigial, the cuff of fierce proclivities
capable, still, of striking home –
dire deeds, dread devices to carry them through.

'Who hears or reads of That, *shall publish* Thee': *Print, Transmission, and the King's Book*

MICHAEL DURRANT

Eikon Basilike, subtitled *The Portraiture of his Sacred Majesty in his Solitudes and Sufferings*, was first published by royalist printer-publisher, Richard Royston (1601-1686), on 30 January 1649, the day of Charles I's (1600-1649) execution at Whitehall. The text, which purports to contain Charles's prayers, devotional reflections, and first-person descriptions of his actions both in the lead up to, and during, the British Civil Wars (1642-1648), soon became a 'gloomy bestseller', capitalising on a deep public interest in Charles's last testimony.[1] Early editions of *Eikon Basilike* contained a frontispiece, title page, a contents page, and a total of twenty-eight headed chapters charting events from the king's perspective over an eight-year period, from 1640 through to 1648.[2] Subsequent editions saw the text published in multiple sizes and rubricated formats, including pocket editions, which encouraged various levels of user interface with the martyred king's testimony.[3] The 'king's book,' as it became known, was also printed abroad, and the text was 'translated into the most spread Languages', including Dutch, French, German and Danish.[4]

Although royalist commentators idealised Charles as the text's 'onely Author', the *Eikon* was in fact the product of collaborative labour, which united a variety of agents in the construction and maintenance of the king's posthumous pres-

1 Barbara Ravelhofer, 'Shirley's Tragedies', in Ravelhofer (ed.), *James Shirley and Early Modern Theatre: New Critical Perspectives* (Oxon and New York: Routledge, 2017), 86-107 (p. 87).

2 Robert Wilcher, '*Eikon Basilike*: The Printing, Composition, Strategy, and Impact of "The King's Book"', in *The Oxford Handbook of Literature and the English Revolution*, ed. by Laura Lunger Knoppers (Oxford: Oxford University Press, 2012), 289-308 (p. 289).

3 See Thomas N. Corns, 'The Early Modern Search Engine', in Neil Rhodes and Jonathan Sawday (eds.), *The Renaissance Computer: Knowledge Technology in the First Age of Print* (London: Routledge, 2000), esp. p. 100.

4 Joseph Jane, *Eikon Aklastos, The Image Unbroken. A Perspective of the Impudence, Falsehood, Vanity, and Prophaneness* (London, 1651), p. 4.

ence, including publishers, printers, editors, other book-trade distributors, and readers.[5] Their contributions meant that the *Eikon* took on 'a life of its own as a material object', and the scope of its transmission in print has since been described as 'unprecedented'.[6] Indeed, thirty-five editions of the work (50, 000 copies) were printed in England by the end of 1649, and the text was reissued throughout the Interregnum and Restoration periods.

The text had 'a profound effect on its royalist readers', giving the absent king a powerful material presence, but the book's commercial success must also be down to the *Eikon's* openness to re-workings and re-interpretation.[7] In the weeks, months, and years following the regicide, textual consumption and redeployment meant that the *Eikon* became an ever more complex royalist vehicle, transposed into verse, revised and reproduced with additional material, and parts of the text were extracted, repackaged, and published in separate editions. While the text's Greek title gestures towards the notion of a singular 'royal image', and despite the fact that the king's book was often venerated as a textual embodiment of 'soliditie', the *Eikon* generated a range of popular textual spin-offs that offered royalist readers a reassuring, although plural and multifaceted, vision of the king, and a means by which they could fashion and sustain their own royalist identities in his absence.[8]

With this in mind, this essay will outline some of the ways in which early and modern readers have conceptualised, regarded, and even 'fetishized', *Eikon Basilike*.[9] It acknowledges the complexity and contingency of the aesthetic experiences the book offers its readers, as well as its highly mediated status as a textual phenomenon in print culture. It examine the meanings and symbolisms that have been attached to the king's book, and I think about these interpretations in relation to the protocols of contemporary book history and interrelated field of print culture studies, which has stressed the 'social processes' of a text's

5 Anon, *The Princely Pellican. Royall Resolves Presented in Sundry Choice Observations, Extracted from His Majesties Divine Meditations* (London, 1649), p. 25.

6 Elizabeth Sauer, *'Paper-Contestations' and Textual Communities in England, 1640-1675* (Toronto: University of Toronto Press, 2005), p. 65; Elizabeth Skerpan Wheeler, '*Eikon Basilike* and the Rhetoric of Self-Representation', in *The Royal Image: Representations of Charles I*, ed. by Thomas N. Corns (Cambridge: Cambridge University Press, 1999), pp. 122-40 (p. 123).

7 Jim Daems and Holly Faith Nelson, 'Introduction', in Daems and Nelson (eds.), *Eikon Basilike, with Selections from Eikonoklastes* (Plymouth: Broadview Editions, 2006), pp. 13-40 (p. 14).

8 Joseph Jane, *Salmasius his Dissection and Confutation of the Diabolical Rebel Milton* (London, 1660), p. 4.

9 Bianca F-C. Calabresi, '"His Idoliz'd Book": Milton, Blood, and Rubrication', in Heidi Brayman, Jesse M. Lander, and Zachary Lesser (eds.), *The Book in History, the Book as History: New Intersections of the Material Text. Essays in Honor of David Scott Kastan* (New Haven, CT: Yale University Press, 2016), pp. 207-232 (p. 209).

'transmission'.[10] Ultimately, I am interested in how the *Eikon* moved: both in terms of the affective responses it elicited from its readers, and also how it was transmitted between manuscript and print, between persons and places. In doing so, this essay will bring to the fore important paradigms about the manipulability of print, and the participatory nature of early modern authorship and textual production.

I. 'The Royal Plea'

Eikon Basilike only achieved the form of the king's textual farewell after a long gestation period, beginning as far back as 1642. As Wilcher suggests, the *Eikon* probably did not begin its life as a memorial to Charles the martyr, but as an intervention into a 'battle for political power that had not yet been irrecoverably lost.'[11] He argues that when Charles first came up with the idea of 'drawing up a vindication of his actions in 1642', and even when he 'set about putting his papers in order in 1647', he could not have known that 'publication would coincide with the final bloody act' of regicide.[12] Indeed, up until at least December 1648, the text's working title was 'The Royal Plea'.[13] The title was changed to *Eikon Basilike* just a few weeks before the king's execution, highlighting how temporary and flexible the book's meanings were, and the extent to which the *Eikon's* final shape was 'a process of comparison and improvement' in response to the king's changing fortunes.[14]

It is now considered likely that the documents that make up the *Eikon* were based, at least in part, on existing materials composed and/or read by Charles I. Dr. John Gauden (1605-1662), the king's chaplain, functioned as one of the text's editors and its ghost writer, and he is seen as having been partly responsible for compiling, revising, and repackaging the text.[15] Despite the collaborative nature of the its composition, the published text, in emphasizing Charles's

10 Donald F. McKenzie, *Bibliography and the Sociology of Texts* (Cambridge: Cambridge University Press, 1999), p. 13.

11 Wilcher, 'What was the King's Book for?: The Evolution of *Eikon Basilike*', *The Yearbook of English Studies* 21 (1991), pp. 218-28 (p. 227).

12 Wilcher, 'What was the King's Book for?', p. 227.

13 See David Grey, 'Prayer and the Sacred Image: Milton, Jeremy Taylor, and the *Eikon Basilike*', in *Milton Quarterly* 46:1 (2012), pp. 1-14 (p. 1).

14 Lotte Hallinga, 'Printing', in Hallinga and J.B. Trapp (eds.), *The Cambridge History of the Book in Britain, Vol. III: 1400-1557* (Cambridge: Cambridge University Press, 1999), pp. 65-108 (p. 91).

15 See Kathleen Lynch, 'Religious Identity, Stationers' Company Politics, and Three Printers of *Eikon Basilike*', *Papers of the Bibliographical Society of America* 101 (2007), pp. 285-312.

'*Solitudes*' on its title-page, worked hard to position readers as paratextual witnesses to, and participants in, the unmediated 'private reflections' and 'impartial thoughts' of the king.[16] Charles's 'Incomparable Book' was even read as a compendium of the king's 'Solliloquies', a configuration that grants a degree of 'veracity' to Charles's meditations, since it implies that the *Eikon* contains thoughts uttered aloud without the speaker having to tailor that address to suit a particular audience.[17] As Sharon Achinstein puts it, *Eikon Basilike* 'appeared as a private document in every way', from its deployment of the genre of the letter, to the presence of the king's personal prayers, which conclude each chapter.[18] The text 'spoke a private language' in its heavy use of first-person pronouns, and occasionally even in its published format, as many early editions of the *Eikon* were transmitted as duodecimos, 'tiny books that could be slipped into one's pockets'.[19]

The king's book was also situated as, to quote from the text's long title again, a '*Sacred*' text. The notion of the *Eikon* as a holy or divine entity finds thematic parallel in the text, where Charles draws comparisons between his own sufferings and the sufferings of Christ.[20] Charles I, generously depicted in William Marshall's (*fl.* 1617-1649) frontispiece engraving as an overtly Christ-like monarch, kneeling at a basilica, is presented throughout the text as 'a king more sinned against than sinning', and a rock in a tempestuous sea of radical rebellion.[21] Indeed, Charles-the-narrator frequently represents himself as an emblem of fixity and stability, as 'An Anchor, a Harbour rather, to these tossed and weather-beaten kingdoms' (*EB*, p.193). Revealingly, Charles also posits his writings within the contexts of the theatre, describing the nation's situation, in which 'Protestant Subjects [. . .] have taken up Arms against their King, a Protestant', as being akin to an 'Act' in a 'Tragedy' (*EB*, p.74). This trope gestures poignantly towards Charles's ending, but it can also serve as a metaphor in miniature for the *Eikon*, which, like drama, 'shows rather than tells'.[22]

16 Daems and Nelson, eds., *Eikon Basilike*, pp. 183-4. All further references to *Eikon Basilike* are taken from this edition, and will be provided in the text.

17 David Lloyd, *Memoires of the Lives, Actions, Sufferings and Deaths* (London, 1668), p. 221; Helmer J. Helmers, *The Royalist Republic* (Cambridge: Cambridge University Press, 2015), p. 119.

18 Sharon Achinstein, *Milton and the Revolutionary Reader* (Princeton, NJ: Princeton University Press, 1994), p. 134.

19 Ibid.

20 See Erin Murphy, *Familial Forms: Politics and Genealogy in Seventeenth-Century English Literature* (Newark, MD: University of Delaware Press, 2011), esp. pp. 93-6.

21 David Lowenstein, *Milton and the Drama of History: Historical Vision, Iconoclasm, and the Literary Imagination* (Cambridge: Cambridge University Press, 1990), p. 54.

22 Helmers, p. 119.

Marshall's portrait of Charles in solitary prayer prepared readers for the experience offered by the book, in which Charles's imprisonment and separation from his family, his chaplains, and his people, is offered as a source and sign of parliamentarian 'Unchristianness', and the king's own 'Conscience and Constancy' (*EB*, pp.169-70). However, the visual image of Charles was only one in a range of (para)textual apparatuses deployed to fashion a sense of personal interaction between the reader and the text's absent author. For instance, the edition of the *Eikon* issued by William Dugard (1606-62) in March 1649 supplied readers with a range of previously unpublished materials, including a letter written from the Prince of Wales to his father, an epigraph on the king's death, as well as a collection of aphorisms related to the book. Supplementary prayers, said to have been composed by Charles before his execution and delivered to William Juxon (1582-1663), Charles's chaplain during his time of imprisonment, were also attached to early editions of the *Eikon*. Such accretions helped to authorize, in Lois Potter's words, open access to 'the secret cabinet of the king's heart', commodifying Charles I's status not only as a self-sacrificing monarch, but as a paternal father-figure, and even a relatable 'Man' (*EB*, p.195).[23]

Just as God's mercy is, according to Charles, '*full of variety*' (*EB*, p.135), the same might be said of the king's book, a text that 'operated on a variety of levels and presented a variety of themes.'[24] On the one hand, the *Eikon* can be read as a deeply conservative politico-religious manifesto in support of the monarchical status quo, a text that fetishizes formal societal decorum, political tradition, and non-resistance to the 'enjoyments which the Laws have assigned to [England's monarchy]' (*EB*, p.191). On the other, the text sanctioned readers' defiance of parliamentarian 'Errors and Schisms' (*EB*, p.187), and called on them to undermine the 'pretended Authority' (*EB*, p.211) of parliament by reading, and transmitting, *Eikon Basilike*. This sense of vacillation between a conservative impulse – bound up in the *Eikon's* nostalgic call for readers to 'remember' the 'happy' reigns of '*Q. Elizabeth*' and James I (ibid.) – and royalist action and agency is central to its power. So too is the remarkable fluidity of the text's genre, which takes stylistic cues from a range of popular literary modes.[25] As Daems and Nelson write in their introduction to the text, *Eikon Basilike* is 'a curious hybrid' of 'political memoir, *apologia*, spiritual autobiography, martyrology, hagiography, meditation, and Psalter.'[26] The text's hybridity is key to its appeal, and it may

23 Lois Potter, *Secret Rites and Secret Writing: Royalist Literature, 1641-1700* (Cambridge: Cambridge University Press, 1989), p. 175.

24 Andrew Lacey, *The Cult of King Charles the Martyr* (Woodbridge: The Boydell Press, 2003), p. 80.

25 See Skerpan Wheeler, '*Eikon Basilike* and the Rhetoric of Self-Representation', pp. 122-140.

26 *Eikon Basilike* (2006), p. 23.

also have been a source of interpretive ambiguity, since the text can be read from any number of vantage points, including as a 'literary work, a series of religious meditations, or a political tract'.[27]

II. 'thy covering to display'

Occasionally, commentators acknowledged the difficulty they had in fully capturing, and transmitting, the book's perceived force. For example, in Abraham Wright's (1611-1690) royalist miscellany, *Parnassus Biceps* (1656), the poem 'Upon the Kings-Book bound up in a Cover' responds to the *Eikon* by acknowledging the poet's inability to provide a satisfactory response. Wright admits that no 'Tongues' can 'add glory' to an already perfect creation: readers are struck 'Speechlesse' by a 'book / So great'. The poet's speechlessness turns to praise of the *Eikon's* 'covering', rather than its contents, which is depicted as being akin to the 'masks of Ladies', though in a violent twist, one that has been 'purpled' with Charles's 'gore'.[28] That the default response to the *Eikon* is to react to its 'Garments' rather than the body of the book beneath might underscore the problem of how, exactly, readers were to respond to a text in which genres mixed so freely. It is, in this example, practically regarded as compulsory that we read the king's book by its cover. Perhaps, however, the issue is even more fundamental: how could royalist readers celebrate, without undermining, a 'bless'd' object that parallels only 'the Gosple', and one that, by extension, had its origins in the rupture of regicide? To narrativize the *Eikon's* 'beauty' is to evoke the 'blood' that was spilt in its creation; at the same time, to 'commend' an already 'glorious' and 'hallowed' textual entity threatens to turn a rarified 'Jewel' into a simple 'Book'.[29]

As I discuss below, the *Eikon* was sometimes figured as a text that could speak, engaging in a self-perpetuating dialogue with its readers. Here, however, we find the rhetoric of speechlessness – the inability to articulate loss, for example, or desire, or praise – which was a common trope in literatures of the period.[30] Speechlessness was also rightly understood as a medical condition – aphonia – arising 'from the *Palsie*', or drunkenness, and it was sometimes also

27 Potter, *Secret Rites*, p. 170.

28 Abraham Wright, *Parnassus Biceps. Or, Severall Choice Pieces of Poetry* (London, 1656), pp. 54-5.

29 Wright, pp. 54-5.

30 For more on the rhetoric of speechlessness and its relation to trauma in early modern literature, see Thomas P. Anderson, *Performing Early Modern Trauma from Shakespeare to Milton* (Oxon and New York: Routledge, 2006), esp. 169-206.

framed 'as a species of trauma, both individual and communal.'[31] In this context, Wright's speechlessness in the face of the *Eikon* might find equivalence in the 'speechlesse' crowds that witnessed Charles's execution; those whose desire '[t]o speak' was inhibited by the traumatic sight of the king's corpse, which apparently left onlookers 'Thunder-struck and dumbe'.[32]

At the same time, however, Wright's language curiously parallels contemporary evaluations of the 1611 King James Bible (henceforth KJB). Henry Vaughan (1621-1695), for example, describes the KJB as 'life's guide!', but, echoing Wright, the text also tests the limits of his/our language, since the Bible's '*effects* no tongue can tell'. In fact, Vaughan suggests that human agency is unseated by the KJB, an object that possesses its own 'searching ray' that can 'woo' the 'eye': in other words, it is the Bible, and the Bible alone, that has the capacity to (seductively) read you.[33] Similarly, Wright picks up on the concept of the textual-ocular 'ray', which emanates from Charles's 'rare piece' to meet, and shape, the eye of the beholder.[34] In doing so, he redeploys aspects of early modern ocular theory, particularly those in accordance with the Aristotelian view that objects, such as planets, mirrors, death shrouds, and here, books, could transmit their qualities (good or bad) through the eyes, invisibly 'binding' men to that object in a one-way contract.[35] The failure of the tongue in the face of the *Eikon* (and the KJB) can therefore be read as an expression of the text's divine capacity to visually *bind* the observer to its contents.

It is also linked to prevailing Protestant attitudes to reading, and to the question of how best to read, and write about, the Word. While reading was a central activity in the Protestant project, it also produced a range of 'anxieties' related to correct 'reading protocols'.[36] In particular, the 'early modern emphasis on scripture's seamless unity', and the Bible's 'single divine authorship', meant that, for many devotional writers, to write about the Bible by focusing on, or

31 Joannes Jonstonus, *The Idea of Practical Physick in Twelve Books* (London, 1657), p. 60; Ernest B. Gilman, *Plague Writing in Early Modern England* (Chicago, IL: Chicago University Press, 2009), p. 54.

32 John Cleveland, *Monumentum Regale or a Tombe, Erected for that Incomparable and Glorious Monarch, Charles the First* (London, 1649), p. 31.

33 Henry Vaughan, 'To the Holy Bible', in Alan Rudrum (ed.), *Henry Vaughan: The Complete Poems* (London: Penguin Books, 1976), pp. 310-11.

34 Wright, pp. 54-5.

35 Thijs Weststeijn, '"Painting's Enchanting Poison": Artistic Efficacy and the Transfer of Spirits', in *Spirits Unseen: The Representation of Subtle Bodies in Early Modern European Culture*, ed. by Christine Göttler and Wolfgang Neuber (Leiden: Brill, 2008), (pp. 144-5).

36 Jacqueline Pearson, 'Dreadful News from Wapping (and Elsewhere): Gender, Reading and the Supernatural in Early Modern England', *Women's Writing* 17:1 (2010), pp. 147-65 (p. 148, p. 154).

quoting, specific scriptural passages threatened to infringe upon the text's divine totality.[37] This same problem appears to inflect Wright's anxiously 'Speechlesse' state, since he flags up the *Eikon's* logocentric, scripture-like unity in the suggestion that 'every leafe's a library / Fil'd with choice Gems'.[38] Rather than isolate particular internal features of the text, then, Wright's job is to showcase the *Eikon*, to 'display' its external dimensions, such as its bindings, to which readers can pay 'harmelesse' adoration.[39]

The *Eikon* was certainly an object to be adored, and it was venerated as a '*Living Memoriall*', and even as a holy relic.[40] Sometimes, alleged remnants of the king's body were literally made into the book's binding: copies of the text were privately bound in scraps of Charles I's hair and his bloody clothing, interwoven with intricate gold and silver thread designs.[41] Such practices draw attention not only to the way in which Protestant culture appropriated forms of Catholic devotion, but to the way in which the binding itself becomes the space for the reader's dramatic worship. It is where readers could materially mark out their relations to the *Eikon*, and by binding the book, they articulate how the book has bound them.

III. 'Who hears or reads of *That*, shall publish *Thee*'

By binding the book in bits and pieces of Charles's decapitated corpse, readers could also express a sense of the *Eikon* as an 'incarnational text', one that 'provided a revered, material textual body for Charles I'.[42] The book-as-body was in fact a common metaphor in relation to the *Eikon*. Writing in 1675, for example, James Heath asserted that *Eikon Basilike* was best understood as the physical 'Remains of King Charles the Martyr', an interpretation that sees the king's book actually substituting the decapitated kingly body.[43] This was not, however, a unique formulation in the period. Printed and manuscript royalist elegies dedicated to deceased loyalists frequently reiterated the notion that those

37 Alison Knight, '"This verse marks that": George Herbert's *The Temple* and Scripture in Context', in *The Oxford Handbook of the Bible in Early Modern England: 1530-1700*, ed. by Kevin Killeen, Helen Smith, and Rachel Willie (Oxford: Oxford University Press, 2015), pp. 518-32 (p. 519).

38 Wright, p. 54.

39 Ibid.

40 *The Princely Pellican*, p. 1.

41 See Patricia Fumerton, *Cultural Aesthetics: Renaissance Literature and the Practice of Social Ornament* (Chicago, IL: Chicago University Press, 1991), p. 9.

42 Daems and Nelson, 'Introduction', p. 16.

43 James Heath, *A Chronicle of the Late Intestine War* (London, 1675), p. 236.

identities could live on through textual transmission.[44] A good example of this can be found in Sir William Sanderson's (1586-1676) *Compleat History of the Life and Raigne of King Charles* (1658), which includes a verse dedication to Archbishop William Laud (1573-1645), a senior advisor to Charles I associated with the enforcement of the English *Book of Common Prayer*, who was beheaded in 1645:

> Thy *Book* shall be thy *Statua*, where we finde,
> The Image of thy Nobler part, thy *Minde*;
> Thy *Name* shall be thy *Epitaph*, and he
> Who hears or reads of *That*, shall publish *Thee*[.][45]

The italicized words typographically underscore a range of revealing parallels. Laud is a '*Book*', and that book is a statue, or monument, providing Laud with a durable presence over a long period. Laud's '*Image*' is/as shorthand for his '*Minde*'; the '*Name*' is/as the '*Epitaph*': and in a final logocentric flourish, '*That*', ultimately, equals '*Thee*'. The elegy points towards a highly active, fluid, and interventionist form of reading, bringing together written and oral systems of transmission and situating readers not as passive consumers of the '*Book*', but as key agents in its dissemination.[46]

This notion finds an important locus in Marshall's engraving of Charles I, who is pictured clutching a crown of thorns, his earthly crown at his feet, and his prayerful eyes cast upward to a heavenly crown of immortality. While Charles bemoaned that his children and his people may 'never see My face again' (*EB*, p.191), his frontispiece portrait formed one of the text's most famous paratexts, since it offered the '*Eye*' a unified 'Picture' of monarchy that was, post-regicide, 'Beyond our *Reach*'.[47] Indeed, the *Eikon's* visual iconography, which materially bound the body of the king's words, (re)unified the royal form, giving Charles a 'fixed' visual presence during the Interregnum and beyond.[48] However, the image, like the text as a whole, was defined by movement as much as visual fixity. Marshall's engraving was sold separately, and reproduced in other

44 See Jerome de Groot, *Royalist Identities* (Basingstoke and New York: Palgrave, 2004), esp. pp. 151-53.

45 William Sanderson, *A Compleat History of the Life and Raigne of King Charles from his Cradle to his Grave* (London, 1658), p. 788.

46 For more on this poem, see de Groot, p. 152.

47 F.N.G[entleman], 'Upon His Scared Majesty's Incomparable EIKON BASILIKE'. Cited in Daems and Nelson, *Eikon Basilike*, pp. 215-16 (p. 215).

48 John R. Knott, *Discourses of Martyrdom in English Literature, 1563-1694* (Cambridge: Cambridge University Press, 1993), p. 160.

books; it was also transmitted together with Biblical glosses, and some of the emblems used to frame the kneeling king were reproduced as wearable badges. The frontispiece could in fact be removed and inserted into other books, or pasted to walls.[49] And in their literary tributes to the king's book, royalist writers continued to separate Charles I's image out from the book, treating it as a visual synecdoche of the *Eikon*.

In William Somner's (1598-1669) *The Frontispice* [sic] *of the Kings Book Opened* (1650), which provided readers with an extensive verse panegyric on the *Eikon's* celebrated engraving, the 'Reader' is compelled to 'looke' upon the king's book and its visual representation of Charles's (unharmed, pre-execution) body, since it is through 'His picture' that they will come to 'know him'.[50] Moreover, the power of the image is seen to confer agency upon the spectator, who is driven to 'pray' and 'sing' in response to their visual encounter.[51] In Somner's hands, the image itself – Charles's duplicate 'Front' – is seen to be a deeply transformative prompt for individual action, and it is therefore the indispensable threshold to:

> His *Golden Manual*, so divine, so rare,
> As, save God's booke, admits not compare.
> The Booke of Bookes, so choice (one word for all)
> As e're the Christian world was blest withal!
> This Front is by the Signer, go, enter then;
> Thy Soule nere lodged in a braver Inne[.][52]

The *Eikon* – 'His *Golden Manual*' – is figured as a devotional work, in that it is a book of spiritual instructions and information. This is not just a work that collates Charles's thoughts and feelings, but one that teaches and guides the reader. In this way, the king's book is only comparable with the KJB – 'God's booke', or the 'Booke of Bookes' – and like the KJB translation, *Eikon Basilike* is not something that you passively read. Recalling the KJB's 1611 title-page engraving, which featured apostles seated in an arcade, and echoing the preliminary poems in George Herbert's (1593-1633) *The Temple* (1633), which invite readers to conceptualise 'the book as architecture', the *Eikon* is similarly charac-

49 See Kevin Sharpe, '"An Image Doting Rabble": The Failure of Republican Culture in Seventeenth-Century England', in *Refiguring Revolutions: Aesthetics and Politics from the English Revolution to the Romantic Revolution*, ed. by Sharpe and Steven N. Zwicker (Los Angeles: The University of California Press, 1998), pp. 25-56 (p. 33).

50 William Somner, *The Frontispice of the Kings Book Opened* (London, 1650), p. 3.

51 Ibid., p. 4.

52 Ibid.

terized as a building – an 'Inne' – that readers are encouraged to 'enter'.[53] The noun 'go' reinforces this sense of reading as movement, or reading as a point of departure, and perhaps by entering the book, the book enters, and therefore produces, its readers.

IV. 'By Heav'n 'tis Licenc'd'

This form of embodied reading reinforces the *Eikon's* status as a 'divine' book, but it also sanctions the text's circumvention of laws related to the licensing and censorship of print products: 'By Heav'n 'tis Licenc'd,' writes Somner, 'and may not goe downe.'[54] What is particularly striking here is Somner's juggling of the *Eikon's* status as a transcendent work of devotion, as a visual, architectural, and interactive structure that should be read in relation to the KJB, with technical jargon associated with the printing trade, embedded within the term 'Licenc'd'.

The transmission and re-transmission of printed books in early-modern England was (technically, at least) constrained by a set of legal controls. Since 1557, when Mary I granted the Stationers' Company a charter for incorporation, Company members were meant to 'enter' their rights in a text or 'copy' in the 'Hall Book' or, as it is more commonly known today, the Stationers' Register. From 1588, members would pay sixpence per entry, or sometimes less when registering pamphlets and ballads. Entry in the Stationers' Register, which was given further impetus during Charles I's reign via a Star Chamber decree of 1637, constituted a form of proto-copyright, granting the stationer responsible for registering the text a legal license over that textual property. It nominally functioned as a form of censorship, too, since in order to make an entry in the Stationers' Register with one of the Company's Masters, Wardens, or Assistants, a text had to be externally approved as being free from seditious material, and the manuscript decked with an official 'imprimatur'. While the laws and regulations associated with press licenses were 'not fully comprehensive', the regulation and licensing of printed books was still a matter of controversy.[55] Central to the debate was the question of who had the authority to dictate ownership rights, and to authorise which texts could or could not be transmitted in print. Was it the crown, who had the executive privilege of God's

53 Adam Smyth, *Material Texts in Early Modern England* (Cambridge: Cambridge University Press, 2018), p. 49.

54 Somner, p. 4.

55 Joad Raymond, *Pamphlets and Pamphleteering in Early Modern Britain* (Cambridge: Cambridge University Press, 2003), p. 70.

ordination, or the corporate body of the Stationers' Company? This became a pressing issue following 'the demise of state mechanisms for regulating printing in 1641', and the introduction of a Parliamentary and Presbyterian licensing system in 1643, which placed increasing pressure on, and threatened to 'derail', the oppositional royalist press.[56]

Somner articulates a sense of the king's book as having stood apart from that fray, breaching systems of control within and without the Stationers' Company. The king's book was 'Licenc'd' by 'Heav'n' and therefore authorised and transmitted by an alternative godly (Anglican) authority. But that is, of course, not the full story of the text's transmission. Printed texts, as John Thompson reminds us, exist in the 'material world and [are] subject to human agency'.[57] Although Somner idealises the king's book as a godly production, a book imbued with the king's divine right, he does not fully gloss the economic and social foundations of the *Eikon's* realisation. Somner suggests that the collapse of royal regulations over the press did nothing to suppress the king's book, since the *Eikon* gained its '*Imprimatur*' and approval through its compassionate readership, whose purchasing power is seen to have seriously negated parliamentarian efforts to control the book's diffusion.[58] Thus, while Somner's interpretation calls attention to early modern stereotypes associated with 'the press as a God-given instrument', it also points us towards the action and agency of readers in the *Eikon's* post-1649 survival.[59]

V. '*Echo*'

Some readers may well have consumed the *Eikon* in their own spaces of solitude, but the text's rhetorical force lay in its status as a speech-act. It gave posthumous life and material shape to words that the king had '*intended to speak*', but '*against reason was hindered to show*' (*EB*, p.211). The text therefore offered

56 Sabrina A. Baron, 'Licensing Readers, Licensing Authorities in Seventeenth-Century England', in *Books and Readers in Early Modern England: Material Studies*, ed. by Jennifer Andersen and Elizabeth Saur (Philadelphia: University of Pennsylvania Press, 2002), pp. 217-42 (p. 217); Randy Robertson, *Censorship and Conflict in Seventeenth-Century England: The Subtle Art of Division* (University Park: The Pennsylvania State University Press, 2009), p. 70.

57 Simon Eliot, 'Introduction', in *Books and Bibliography: Essays in Commemoration of Don McKenzie*, ed. by John Thompson (Wellington: Victoria University Press, 2002), pp. 7-19 (p. 13).

58 Somner, p. 4.

59 Elizabeth Eisenstein, *Divine Art, Infernal Machine: The Reception of Printing in the West from First Impressions to the Sense of an Ending* (Philadelphia: The University of Pennsylvania Press, 2011), p. 34.

readers 'what many could think the Commonwealth was denying them: a voice'.[60] The *Eikon* was, in fact, seen to have a profound oral potential. We know, for example, that landowning royalists bought the *Eikon* in bulk and distributed the text freely amongst aristocratic networks, who then had the text read aloud to their servants and tenants.[61] This ensured that the king's book reached literate and non-literate readers beyond the city of London, but it also meant that those reading (or hearing) the text were together participating in its transmission, one that draws attention to the relationship between speaker, hearer, and *Eikon's* subject matter.

In the anonymous 1659 pamphlet, *The Faithful, yet Imperfect, Character of a Glorious King*, Charles's 'never-to-be-paralleld BOOK' is seen to house the dead king's 'speaking Ghost, the Echo of his Life and Death'. The king's 'BOOK' – the stylized capitalisation capturing a sense of the *Eikon* as a fixed, monolithic product – is represented as a haunted architectural structure, a kind of tomb, and also a kind of ghost story of the martyred king, whose voice can be heard as 'Echo', or oral repetition. Charles's ghost speaks, and we are meant to hear 'those sad, sweet Meditations'.[62] This is not impossible, since the *Eikon* was often read aloud, and parts of it were even sung.[63] In consuming the book in such a way, those mourning for the loss of a king could literally echo their monarch's last words by speaking or singing them. If royalist readers were to read the *Eikon* 'o're and o're', as the author of 'An epigraph upon King CHARLS' (1649) suggests, a still more interactive and reiterative model of reading emerges, one that pulls explicitly on Protestant reading protocols, which promoted 'reading scriptures from beginning to end, and then starting again'.[64]

The idea of Charles's voice as '*Echo*' was picked up elsewhere, and contrasted favourably with the king's living '*voice*', which, in being 'silenc'd' by 'death', is painted as having not possessed the same dynamism as the textual '*Manual*' that outlived him.[65] If the acoustic effect of the echo activates associations of a 'lurking and invisible vocal presence', then these allusions together capture a sense of the king's book as having the capacity to transmit in furtive, and poten-

60 Skerpan Wheeler, p. 132.

61 Jason Peacey, *Print and Public Politics in the English Revolution* (Cambridge: Cambridge University Press, 2013), pp. 80-81.

62 Anon, *The Faithful, yet Imperfect, Character of a Glorious King* (London, 1659), p. 17.

63 Richard Helgerson, 'Milton Reads the King's Book', *Criticism* 29 (1987), pp. 1-25 (p. 12).

64 I.H., 'An Epigraph upon King CHARLS', in Anon, *A Perfect Copie of Prayers, used by His Majestie in the Time of His Sufferings* (London, 1649), p. 314; Femke Molekamp, *Women and the Bible in Early Modern England: Religious Reading and Writing* (Oxford: Oxford University Press, 2013), p. 61.

65 Anon, '*Upon His Sacred Majesty's incomparable* EIKON BASILIKE' (1649), cited in Daems and Nelson, *Eikon Basilike*, pp. 215-6.

tially uncontrollable, ways.[66] But the word must also call attention to the *Eikon's* intertextual associations with the KJB, which, much like the king's book, stood in as an '*Eccho* out of Gods love'; 'a redoubling, a repeating [. . .] of the same voice'.[67] The king's book is, in fact, heavy with Biblical echoes, interpolating quotations into nearly all of its chapters. Charles quotes or alludes to David, Job, the crucified Christ, and Samson, and these scriptural voices 'merge' with the words of Charles and therefore give vital spiritual shape to his narrative voice.[68]

As John Milton (1608-1674) recognised in his *Eikonoklastes* (1649) – meaning 'Image Breaker' or 'Smasher' – one of the king's supplementary prayers, entitled 'A *Prayer* in time of *Captivity*', and beginning '*O Powerful and Eternal God!*' (*EB*, p.205), was 'stolen word for word from the mouth of a Heathen Woman': Princess Pamela, who appears in book 3, chapter 6 of Sidney's *The Countess of Pembroke's Arcadia* (1590).[69] This disclosure strengthened Milton's polemical goal, which was to represent the *Eikon* as an inauthentic work, and one characterised by a 'Pageantry of some Twelfth-night's entertainment at *Whitehall*''.[70] However, his revelation, while useful for a Commonwealth eager to unsettle Charles's status as the *Eikon's* sole originator, should not stand in as a source and sign of royalist creative idleness. It is no coincidence that *Eikon Basilike* was borrowing from a text that had, by the mid-1640s, become a touchstone for a number of 'disenfranchised' royalist writers, who similarly allied themselves with the nostalgic 'world of chivalric romance [Sidney] had described.'[71] Indeed, we now understand that Charles's '*Golden Manual*'' was not 'rare', as Somner put it, at least in the sense that it was wholly unique or even original. The 'power of the king's self-representation [. . .] lies precisely in its lack of originality', in its deployment of 'readily recognizable models'; in its echoing of former works (Biblical or literary), which had come to take a central place in royalist forms of self-fashioning.[72] The claims made in a number of the above extracts, concerning the *Eikon's* rarity and its incomparability, may in

66 John Hollander, *The Figure of the Echo: A Mode of Allusion in Milton and After* (Los Angeles: University of California Press, 1981), p. 2.

67 Jakob Böhme, *Mysterium Magnum, or, An Exposition of the First Book of Moses called Genesis* (London, 1656), p. 57; John Donne, *LXXX Sermons Preached by that Learned and Reverend Divine, Iohn Donne* (London, 1640), p.163.

68 Skerpan Wheeler, p. 126.

69 John Milton, *Eikonoklastes in Answer to a Book Intitl'd Eikon Basilike* (London, 1649), in Daems and Nelson, *Eikon Basilike*, pp. 219-83 (p.236). All other citations from *Eikonoklastes* are taken from this edition.

70 Milton, p. 224.

71 Stephen B. Dobranski, *Readers and Authorship in Early Modern England* (Cambridge: Cambridge University Press, 2005), p. 75.

72 Skerpan Wheeler, p. 128.

this context be a wilful misreading of a book that demanded to be understood in relation to other texts rather than in isolation.

VI. 'Thou art so hard a Text'

Early readers often marked up their copies of the *Eikon* with exactly this in mind, leaving behind traces of the way in which they understood the king's book's relationships with other texts, and the lives of those responsible for them. For example, in a 1649 edition of the *Eikon*, printed by Henry Hills (c. 1624-1688/9) and now kept at the John Ryland's Library, Manchester (R88125), there is evidence of a late seventeenth-century reader isolating and copying out a long passage from Clement Walker's (1595-1651) *History of Independency, Part II*, and introducing that passage into the title page's verso leaf in their copy of the king's book.[73] The fourteen-line manuscript transcription comes originally from the 1660 edition of Walker's *Anarchia Anglicana* (first published in 1649), which provides a potted history of the *Eikon*, described as 'a Phoenix out of his Majesties ashes, that most excellent issue of his brain'.[74] The commonplaced passage has Walker describe Charles as 'more than conqueror of his enemies in his rare Christian patience', and he suggests that the 'very reading' of the *Eikon* 'aggravateth our loss of so rare & excellent a prince'. The book's suppression under Cromwell is also discussed: 'Herod [. . .] never persecuted Christ in his Swadling Clothes with more industrious malice [than] ye antimonarchical & Independent Faction did this book in ye Presses & Shops'. The reader-editor then goes on to contextualise this material with an eight-line biographical note, stating that the author of the transcribed passage, Walker, had in his own lifetime been a religious radical, and 'very zealous against ye King', but that the regicide, and the *Eikon*, had brought him to the royalist side, for which he was committed to the Tower. The biographical snapshot ends by noting that Walker died there in 1651.[75]

By reading the manuscript extract from *Anarchia Anglicana* and the bio-bibliographical note in conjunction with one another, a narrative of conversion as well as martyrdom emerges, one that emphasizes how the *Eikon* could affect

73 [John Gauden], *Eikon basilike: The Pourtraicture of His Sacred Majestie in His Solitudes and Sufferings* (John Rylands Library, Manchester), ESTC r13359.

74 For the passage's printed source, see Clement Walker, *Anarchia Anglicana, or, The History of Independency. The Second Part* (London, 1660), pp. 138-39.

75 For more on Walker, see David Underdown, 'Walker, Clement (*d.* 1651)', *Oxford Dictionary of National Biography*, Oxford University Press, 2004 [http://www.oxforddnb.com/view/article/28473].

and change its readers, and also how its readers took on some of the martyrological attributes of the dead king. Indeed, Walker's own reading of the *Eikon*, in which he emphasizes the text's ability to 'teach', finds a corollary in this reader's note on Walker's own transformation. This act of commonplacing also highlights how seventeenth-century printed texts could be 'reworked' within different contexts.[76] Indeed, this reader's use of the *Eikon* evidences not a sense of either the king's book or *Anarchia Anglicana* as fixed or finished objects, but as texts in a dialogue that can be elucidated and extended through the work of extraction and rearrangement. Further, the manuscript copy and its accompanying note suggest a reader comfortable with the idea that printed books allude to, and make their meaning from, other printed texts and the lives associated with those texts.

The next example is taken from a 1649 anonymous elegy to the king's book entitled simply, 'Another'. Here, the prerequisite for readerly encounters with the absent king is an ability to spell, to understand words, to know how to articulate and intonate them. The poem suggests that method of reading Charles-as-text is, in fact, a lesson in literacy:

> He that can spel a Sigh, or read a Tear,
> Pronounce amazement, or Accent wild Fear:
> Having all Grief by Heart, He, only He
> Is fit to write and read thy Elegy
> Unvalued CHARLS: Thou art so hard a Text,
> Writ in one Age, not understood i'th' next.[77]

In this example, the written word is seen to produce, to multiply, the affective responses that they signify: sighing, crying, amazement and fear are to be read, to be said, but also to be felt. Reading is also represented as a form of writing; we 'write' even as we 'read' the 'Unvalued CHARLS'. Following on from this we find those final two complex lines: 'Thou art so hard a Text, / Writ in one Age, not understood i'th' next.' Charles, then, is text, the body and the book are elided. In describing Charles as 'a Text', the poem recalls the Latin *texere*, which, as Donald McKenzie points out, infers a 'woven state', a 'web or texture of materials'.[78] To view Charles as 'Text' therefore diverts us from a sense of him as being made up of 'any one substance or any one form'.[79] But crucially

76 Stephen Colclough, *Consuming Texts: Readers and Reading Communities, 1695-1870* (London: Palgrave, 2007), p. 30.

77 Anon, *A Perfect Copie of Prayers, used by His Majestie in the Time of His Sufferings* (London, 1649), p. 315.

78 McKenzie, pp. 13-14.

79 Ibid., p. 14.

he is a 'hard' text, signifying either that this textual body is firm, stable and unbreakable, or that Charles-as-text is difficult to decipher and interpret. The second reading evokes an element of interpretive anxiety that is just about visible in the example by Wright, and it seems appropriate given the final line: Charles is 'Writ in one Age, not understood i'th' next.' Charles has been written in another 'Age', and in another context, but that point of origin, that textual starting point, cannot be adequately returned to.

The same interpretive issue was addressed in other seventeenth-century poems. In John Cleveland's (1613-1658) 'The Kings Disguise', for example, it is argued that when Charles disguised himself as a servant during his escape from Oxford in 1646 he became a 'puzling Portaiture' that was inhabited by 'Riddles', and an obscure 'Text Royall' that is hard to decipher.[80] In Vaughan's 'The King Disguis'd', Charles similarly became a 'Royal Riddle' and 'our Hieroglyphic King' when he concealed himself by casting aside the sartorial signifiers of monarchy.[81] In both instances, Charles's strategic obfuscation of his identity is the source of an interpretive dilemma about what exactly constitutes kingship, and whether royal power is an external or internal quality. Cleveland and Vaughan are also concerned with Charles's status as a highly contested material text, one that, in James Loxley's words, is subject to 'readings and counter-readings', and marked by a certain degree of 'incomprehensibility'.[82] Charles's disguise encapsulates only one element of the king's opacity; another is the degree to which he is subject to the representations of both his friends and foes, 'expository activity' that, during his own lifetime and after, produced multiple versions of the king even, or perhaps especially, in his absence.[83]

'He that can spel' can help to move this idea forward. The poem would go on to appear in the anonymous *Reliquiae Sacrae Carolinae*, printed at The Hague in 1650, and in Richard Head's (1637-1688) biography of a reputed Yorkshire prophetess, *The Life and Death of Mother Shipton,* printed in 1677.[84] However, 1649 did not actually mark this poem's first appearance in print. 'He that can spel' originally appeared in the printed verse miscellany, *Wits Recreations* (1640), and there it went by the title 'On a learned Noble man':

80 *The Kings Disguise* (London, 1646), p. 5.

81 *Thalia Rediviva the Pass-times and Diversions of a Countrey-muse,in choice Poems on Several Occasions* (London, 1678), p. 2.

82 James Loxley, *Royalism and Poetry in the English Civil Wars: The Drawn Sword* (Basingstoke and London: Macmillan, 1997), p. 146, p. 143. Both poems are also usefully discussed in Wilcher's *The Writing of Royalism 1628-1660* (Cambridge: Cambridge University Press, 2001), pp. 246-48.

83 Ibid., p. 147.

84 Anon, *Reliquiae Sacrae Carolinae. Or the Works of that Great Monarch and Glorious Martyr King Charls the I* (The Hague, 1650), p. 353; Richard Head, *The Life and Death of Mother Shipton* (London, 1677), p. 45.

Hee that can reade a sigh and spell a teare,
Pronounce amaze-ment, or accent wilde feare,
Or get all greife by heart, hee, onely hee
Is fit to write, or reade thy Elegye,
Unvalued Lord! that wer't so hard a Text,
Reade in one age and understood i'th' next.[85]

Before 1640, 'On a learned Noble man' had appeared in manuscript, and it was not about King Charles I but instead focused on George Villiers (1592-1628), first Duke of Buckingham, who was stabbed to death in 1628.[86] As such, a poem that, in manuscript, had originally had a specific referent (Villiers) became in print a 'generic' six-line poem to any 'Noble man', a pre-text 'to be appropriated to describe or decry the fall of other eminent figures'.[87] This verse could be 'latched', Adam Smyth says, onto new people and contexts, as appears to have been the case with the martyred king.[88]

As with the above example of a reader extracting material from *Anarchia Anglicana* and copying it into the *Eikon*, the textual recycling of 'He that can spel' signals a participatory model of textual transmission and consumption, and the 'provisionality' of printed forms.[89] For example, in copying out and reproducing 'On a learned Noble man' within a 1649 context, changes have slipped in: this is repetition marked by difference. In the example of 1640 the 'Noble man' can be 'Reade in one age *and* understood i'th' next'; however, when the same verse was applied to the absent Charles that crucial word 'not' slips in towards the middle of the final line. In that earlier 1640 version of the poem, the 'Unvalued' generic 'Lord' is a 'hard [. . .] Text' because the textual lord's posthumous meanings remain consistent, I think, over time, lending that word 'hard' the meanings of rigid and inflexible. When applied to Charles, 'hard' seems to signify the difficulties associated with providing a true reading of the kingly text. The implication appears to be that the establishment of, to borrow a bibliographical phrase, a 'textually pure' text of the king is not possible, since readers, by reading the absent Charles, *re*write him within their historically-specific contexts.[90]

85 Anon, *Wits Recreations. Selected from the Finest Fancies of Modern Muses* (London, 1640), p. 124. According to the ESTC, this text was reprinted at least seven more times between the 1640s and 1680s.

86 See Smyth, '"Reade in one age and understood I'th'next": Recycling Satire in the Mid-Seventeenth Century', *Huntington Library Quarterly* 69:1 (2006), pp. 67-82 (pp. 78-80).

87 Ibid., p. 79.

88 Ibid.

89 Ibid., p. 82.

90 Margreta de Grazia, 'The Essential Shakespeare and the Material Book', in *Shakespeare and the Literary Tradition*, ed. by Stephen Orgel and Sean Kilen (New York, NY: Garland Press, 1999), pp. 51-68 (p. 59).

VII. 'A Prayer made by C.R.'

The British Library's copy of the Yorkshire royalist Sir John Gibson's (1606-1665) quarto manuscript miscellany helps to underscore a sense of Charles as material construction, while also evidencing the deeply transformative ways in which the *Eikon's* readers consumed and redeployed the text.[91] Written while Gibson served a prison sentence for debt in Durham Castle between 1655 and 1660, ADD MS 37719 comprises commonplaced passages from previously published texts, including transcriptions of Herbert's 'Jesu' (fol. 272r) and 'Bitter-sweet' (fol. 272v). There are also a number of examples of transcribed prose, from, for instance, the 1629 Cambridge Bible and the 1639 *Book of Common Prayer*. Gibson's manuscript features examples of original poetry, a drawing in which he appears to have planned the wording on his own memorial stone and the design of his coffin (fol. 249v), and notes addressed to Gibson's son and heir, who is encouraged to 'somee times [. . .] looke upon' the text after his father's death (fol. 5v). The miscellany also includes a selection of clippings appropriated from print products, which have been cut up and pasted into the book at various points, forming a complex *bricolage* where manuscript and print meet. These include a printed ornamental border, which has been carefully cut out from its original setting, and used to frame Gibson's manuscript transcription of a poem (fol. 9v); an engraving of a death and time emblem (fol. 163); an engraving of the bust of Charles II (fol. 185); Charles I's coat of arms, which appeared in some later editions of *Eikon Basilike* (fol. 197v); and a small printed portrait of Charles I (fol. 198).

Gibson's manuscript does not provide a direct commentary on the nature of the king's book, but, as well as cutting and pasting images from the *Eikon*, he does copy out passages from it, and in doing so he offers a particular kind of reading. For example, as he transcribes 'Another PRAYER', which first appeared in Dugard's 15 March 1649 edition of the *Eikon*, he restyles it 'A Prayer made by C.R.' (fol. 262v), which in Dugard's edition begins '*Almighty and most merciful Father, look down upon Me Thy unworthy Servant*' (*EB*, p.206). The prayer's focus is on confession and repentance: Charles admits his '*sinful motions*' and '*unclean thoughts*', and calls on God to show '*compassion*', and to '*purge*' him of his sins (*EB*, pp.206-7). Aside from the change in title, Gibson's transcription is in all other respects a word-for-word reproduction of the prayer as found in *Eikon Basilike*; however, the revised title gives an erroneous impression of that prayer's provenance. 'Another PRAYER' was in fact 'made by' Lewis Bayly

91 British Library, ADD MS 37719.

(*c*.1575-1631), Bishop of Bangor and devotional writer, and it first appeared under the title 'A Prayer for the Morning' in Bayly's highly influential *Practice of Piety* (1612), a Christian self-help book that, amongst other things, featured set prayers for morning, evening, and mealtimes. According to F.F. Madan, a version of this prayer does exist in Charles's hand, and it is dated 1632.[92] Gibson compliments his own transcription of 'A Prayer made by C.R.', which is itself a copy, with a prose entry entitled 'A Confession', which sits on the adjacent recto page, and begins 'Almighty God, father of our Lord Jesus Christ, maker of all things, Judge of all men', and ends with 'to the honour and glory of thy name; through Jesus Christ our Lord' (fol. 236r).

This sixteen-line passage does not appear in the *Eikon*; instead, it has been taken directly from the *Book of Common Prayer* (henceforth BCP), and appears there as a 'General Confession', part of a congregational response to the priest's invitation to receive the Holy Communion. Gibson's decision to situate a transcribed prayer, supposedly written by Charles I, alongside an extract from the traditional Protestant liturgy, can be read as a radical loyalist gesture. In the aftermath of royalist defeat, Gibson's strategic alignment of the two extracts across two facing pages (re)unites monarchical and sacramental authority, and provides a continued textual afterlife for two persecuted books. Indeed, in the very act of copying out material from the *Eikon* and the BCP, Gibson can be seen to conform to an aesthetic ideology that Charles I promoted in the king's book: that the most 'sound and wholesome words' were to be found in pre-existing textual sources (*EB*, p.135).

However, as Helen Wilcox reminds us, 'in the early modern period, to copy was indeed to create.'[93] Gibson has, for example, made significant changes to the wording of the passage originally found in the BCP. As Ramie Targoff notes, the BCP's inclusion of a General Confession before the Sacrament of Holy Confession became 'the crucial utterance of pre-Eucharistic piety', deploying the plural personal pronouns 'our' and 'we' to produce a 'collective voice that does not differentiate among its speakers.'[94] In his transcription, Gibson replaces the original's use of 'we' and 'our' with 'I' and 'my' (fol. 263r), encapsulating a sense of copying as not only absorption but transformation, and as a method of self-fashioning. Gibson's copying constitutes a rewriting of the liturgy's

92 Francis Falconer Madan, *A New Bibliography of the Eikon Basilike of King Charles the First; with a Note on the Authorship* (London: B. Quaritch, 1950), p. 14.

93 Helen Wilcox, '"Sribling under so faire a Coppy": The Presence of Herbert in the Poetry of Vaughan's Contemporaries', *Scintilla* 7 (2003), pp. 185-200 (p. 187).

94 Ramie Targoff, *Common Prayer: The Language of Public Devotion in Early Modern England* (Chicago, IL: Chicago University Press, 2001), p. 33.

emphasis on collective piety and devotion, placing greater emphasis on Gibson's solitary status as an outsider in a republican realm, isolated from family and friends. In this he must be prompted by Charles's performance of martyrdom and isolation in *Eikon Basilike*, which, as discussed, positioned the king's enforced separateness from his people as central paradigm in the book's long title.

The kinds of textual manipulation, reorganization, and adaptation offered in ADD MS 37719, where a passage from the *Eikon* sits alongside printed images, and transcribed extracts from other printed books to which authorial origin is not usually ascribed, highlights print's 'malleability' rather than its fixity, an enactment of the mingling and movement involved in a seventeenth-century text's transmission, as well as Gibson's elastic, rather than prescriptive, attitude to authorship.[95] Indeed, Gibson's strategy of reworking his print sources within a manuscript context, which includes not only copying out and editing pre-existing passages, but cutting and tearing printed pages, literalizes Julia Kristeva's metaphor of the 'mosaic', which she uses to conceptualize the intertextuality and radical instability that mark all forms of literary creation.[96]

However, Gibson's miscellany can, at the same time, be read as a movement against such forms of collage, indicating something more taxonomical. The manuscript features extensive lists of, amongst others, 'the Compilers of the English Common Prayer Booke' (fol. 205), suggesting an interest in tracing textual lineage and origins, as well as a list of England's monarchs, from William the Conqueror (1028-1087) through to Charles I (fol. 185v), underscoring a concomitant concern with bloodlines and patrilineal succession. A short verse note by Gibson, entitled 'To his Booke', tells the manuscript to 'hide' itself and 'lie alone', so that it might be 'safe' from 'hands that teare' (fol. 164), offering a sense of the book as something whose meanings can be preserved, but only by ghettoizing it from potential readers, who, in consuming the book, might deploy Gibson's own strategies of cutting and pasting. If 'Gibson's attitude towards texts and authors was by no means a cultural exception', then that attitude was therefore conflicting, representative, perhaps, of a culture still negotiating with, on the one hand, a sense of the printed page, like the medieval manuscript, as something that requires intervention and that is always changing, and on the other, a desire for textual stability, order, and provenance.[97]

95 Smyth, 'Textual Transmission, Reception and the Editing of Early Modern Texts', *Literature Compass* 1 (2004), pp. 1-9 (p. 2).

96 Julia Kristeva, 'Word, Dialogue and the Novel', in Leon S. Roudiez (ed.), *Desire in Language: A Semiotic Approach to Literature and Art* (New York, NY: Columbia University Press, 1980), p. 66.

97 Smyth, 'Textual Transmission', p. 2.

VIII. 'Bastard Issue'

Eikon Basilike replaced the king's dead body in the same way that the future Charles II was seen to substitute the father, whose 'sparkling fame and Royall Name' lived on in the vessel of the 'sonne'.[98] Such formulations rested on a culturally powerful sense of Charles as father of the book and the English nation, and of the *Eikon* as a form of biological transmission. But, of course, for this to work it was essential to believe that the first-person expressions found in Charles's posthumous text actually came from the martyred king. Parliamentarians, anxious at the book's commercial success, knew this, and in those works that attacked the *Eikon* it was the question of its authorship and origin that took center stage.

The anonymous *Eikon Alethine* (August 1649) was the first parliamentarian pamphlet to cast doubt on Charles's status as the *Eikon's* originator. Its author represents the king's book as a 'black Babe' and a 'Bastard Issue'.[99] By explicitly racializing Charles's 'Bastard Issue' as 'black', *Eikon Alethine* taps into and extends an early-modern belief that associated the origin of racial blackness with Noah's adultery, thus codifying the *Eikon's* own beginnings within the contexts of improper intercourse and illegitimate paternity.[100] Further, *Eikon Alethine's* title-page engraving, which features a hand pulling back a curtain to reveal an unidentified priest or prelate authoring Charles's first-person book, throws into relief a sense of the *Eikon* as a mirage or distraction, a form of fake news designed to obfuscate the king's monarchical failings. The image of the curtain also introduces an idea of the king's book as a stage, and the *Eikon's* first-person emanations as nothing more than a script, one constructed by an off-stage playwright using the figure of the absent king as a convenient mouthpiece.

Milton's *Eikonoklastes*, published by the bookseller and printer, Matthew Simmons (1608-1654), in October 1649, soon followed, and it was in this work that Milton recognized that one of the king's prayers had originally appeared in Sidney's *Arcadia*. According to Susan Howe, the Pamela prayer revelation confronted 'the inauthentic literary work with its beginnings in a breach', and Milton's evidence of forgery became a lightning rod in an authorship debate that raged well into the nineteenth century.[101] This controversy culminated in the

98 Anon, *A Coffin for King Charles: A Crowne for Cromwell: A Pit for the* People (London, 1649), broadsheet.

99 Anon, *Eikon Alethine: The Portraiture of Truth's most Sacred Majesty Truly Suffering, though Not Solely* (London, 1649), frontispiece.

100 See Michael Neill, 'Unproper Beds: Race, Adultery, and the Hideous in *Othello*', *Shakespeare Quarterly* 4:4 (1989), pp. 383-412 (pp. 408-9).

101 Susan Howe, *The Nonconformist's Memorial* (New York, NY: New Directions, 1989), p. 57.

famous bibliographies by Edward Almack (1896) and Madan (1950), which continued the project of compiling 'authoritative texts' to thereby 'discover the original text' of *Eikon Basilike*.[102] However, *Eikon Basilike* ultimately challenges ideologies of textual unity and authorial attribution, highlighting instead the heterogeneous nature of the texts in transmission. As this article has shown, *Eikon Basilike* was produced and transmitted in a culture that understood texts to be mobile, interactive, and active; and, for some readers, it produced deeply affective and relational reading experiences, calling to books beyond it, sometimes in unpredictable ways. The king's book was understood in relation to the visual and the verbal aspects of textual transmission, and the interlinkings between printed texts and lives. Readerly encounters with the *Eikon* also alert us to the collapsing of boundaries between reading, copying, and writing in the seventeenth century, and, in the example taken from Gibson's miscellany, also between manuscript and print. Further, by extracting passages of the *Eikon*, or transcribing passages from other printed books into copies of it, by eulogising the king, and celebrating his textual memorial in verse, or extricating engravings of his image, and by critiquing the text's claims to royal authorship, seventeenth-century readers fragmented the king's book, producing not textual singularity but multiplicity and disparity.

102 Ibid., p. 57-8.

'Temptation of Eve' by Tanja Butler.

PETE MULLINEAUX

Small Hungers

Your bare foot beneath the table brushes mine;
a moment ago they were kicking sand along
the beach – but now we sit in a café,
our heads at rest against a rise of pebbles,
the surf pulled up to our chins –
gulping back the raging sea, each wave
an onslaught of wet delight; clinking of cutlery
like loose metal fastenings on ghostly masts.

In truth it had been a grey affair: low-tide;
cold, misty – the pebbles laced with tar,
so instead we have the comforting heat,
clear water in a jug; having made short work
of the starters, we mull over the main course,
the glare of the white cloth blinding
us to reason – our ravenous toes
scuttling to make sideways love
on the ocean floor.

ROSE FLINT

from ***Lunar Station:***

Icy Salty Cocktail in a Thin Stemmed Glass

I was there, up in the sky with my white suit like a puffed pearl
floating in the black beyond blue where the stars *really* live.
Take a rising line from that stratocumulus and go on, higher
into heaven. I'd walked the angels' own backyard – didn't I say

I saw one for a moment? *poised, thoughtful as stone, considering –*
they say things about light   *a glaze like inverse shadow*
on what can't be   Good stories. Get girls eating out of my hand.

So the moon's for a game and some hard grind, sweat and fuel;
we'll get something from it and afterwards the play.
The best job *out* of this world!
but this girl with her squinny green cat eyes, knowing nothing

and how I felt: ridiculous. To watch her turning a moment
pale face angling away into long heavy hair, dark as obsidian.

I could have got a quick-grow diamond. Laid out cash.
She was just a hippy dropout waiting tables in a TexMex joint
but night after night she wasn't looking.
So what was worth something? Sell-your-soul-time?
I called her over, did the gaze, bought an icy salty cocktail
in a thin-stemmed glass. Then the gift.

And is this the most precious substance on earth?
This moondust, that would float in a lattice of late afternoon sun
streaming in bars through attic blinds like motes we make
from our own beauty, dust of cloud forests, corals, tigers, tribes,
our detritus of skins and light.

He whispers of clever offices and promises
but bites back his breath as she slits her nails into the package
and pours from plastic to palm, intent on the soft black
flecked with ghost threads of glitter or time.

She leans down – goes real slow – and licks –

raises her open mouth closeup to his so he sees
each moondustgrain clear on the universe of her crimson tongue
her stud a crystal engine – as she downs his margarita
with the thirst of the world in her throat.

I've lost the hour, season, reason.
I see her close the midnight curtains and she seems
more lucent than I knew. She is my clock, my revolving world,
I want to touch but I am far away. This earth is void
and she is always distant. I think she has a secret life.

K.V. SKENE

SAD
Seasonal Affective Disorder

Between This World and the Next

this is what we hunger for, need
in our bloodstream, our DNA.
                    This is our god's holy war, scream
of despair, bellow of laughter
                    and none of this matters . . .
In a city like ours February takes over.
No one is exempt.
                    No one escapes
its hungry moon –
bodies hibernate, minds tunnel,
dig cellars and subways and subterranean
super malls –
                    significantly walled and signposted
(although all our tomorrows still arrive
blind and alone)
                    and this is what happens,
will happen
if we let it
                    until March blows in
(sap moon rising)
with seasonally adjusted promises – more sun,
more sky, more space, more sight, more daylight and now we're saving time –
fast-forwarding to spring
                    your wide eyes staring into mine
with what never dies.

K.E. DUFFIN

Mrs. Reed

Your name sways before the wind stirring the cove.
Another spring. The coast has binged on winter.
Along the shore, the sad aftermath of excess.

You are thin as an Egyptian now, your afterlife a lengthening shadow on the dirt drive,
your blackened window a nativity deferred.

All those nights you were alive,
only an orange light framed by soot
declared your seaside vigil.

There and *not there* are nearly twins at the root.
Mrs. Reed, saintly in your roofless tomb,
you point to the wall separating us from nothingness,

point without fingers, hands, arms, womb.
Trees take up your cause, fret
and rustle in the wind,

black, sinuous branchlets
feeling for the face of dawn. (*Not yet.*)

Late Cicada

Whirring down of its serrate spin,
then a long-drawn-out stutter to a stop,
its last syllable undetected in
the heavy silence of a closed shop.

Did the song really end, or flow into a register
beyond our hearing, attain a pitch
for another way of being? Does it stir
the air of a parallel summer, enrich

another year's clandestine hour?
In uneasy stillness, does it persist?
Upstarting in a Florentine tower,
responding like a bold evangelist

is evening's cryptic bell:
Thou hearest the sound thereof, but canst not tell . . .

CHRIS PREDDLE

The Grey Heron

Jacqueline and the grey heron
soak their toes. Each
avails, gives something of her own
on the river beach.

Mag Brook, zigzag brook
turns and turns to ascertain
certainties among those baroque
sententious trees.

Jacqueline the grey heron
rises in the wind like beauty
in the abstracting mind, here now
her ample wingbeat.

Jacqueline on the Hill

On this hill Jacqueline
would lean
as a Moore reclining form
informs composure leaning on her forearm.

Underground her in the alabaster beds
uncarved, the knights and kirtled ladies
waiting for creation call, Form us, lead us
to the sun. Human nature has disturbed us.

Jacqueline would explain,
inclined on her elbow, herself a curve synclined,
would tell them in the bedding planes
how a single form
composed, how made-shapes many-in-one disposed
tell us the real we go towards and from.

W.D. JACKSON

from *Shakespearean Sonnets*

As You Like It – Rosalind

'. . . *the truest poetry is the most feigning.*'
III.iii.16

To pass the time in Arden, I, a boy,
Pretended to be a girl pretending to be
A boy who took a lover's pride and joy
In playing the part of Rosalind, who he –

More so than *I* – both was and will be. Thus
We choose our many roles on Jacques' stage,
And play them as we like them . . . None of us
Survives, except in print. No act, no age

Of man is golden. Winter's biting wind
Howls through the wood – persuades us what we are.
Wrestling with Fortune, we must learn to find
Sermons in stones, music in storm and star.

Ages ago in Arden, I, a boy,
Once played a master's mistress' living joy.

*

The Tempest – Miranda

'Miranda: *O, wonder!*
How many goodly creatures are there here!
How beauteous mankind is! O brave new world,
Which has such people in it!
Prospero: *'Tis new to thee.'*
V.i.181-184

The only men I'd ever seen were old
Or ugly. And my father told of others
Who'd taken all we had. Of men who'd sold
Or fought their fellow-men, or killed their brothers.

Caliban found me bathing once. He swore
He'd take his island back – take all – take me.
My father's Art prevents him – makes him roar
With pain and anger all night long. But he –

Ferdinand – wants to *give* me all he has:
His very life, he says. His father's King
Of Naples; I'll be Queen. My father was
Their enemy, but not now. No loveless thing

Lives long. Love heals the past, outlives the future.
O brave new world, to bring me such a creature!

From Letter to Spirit: Henry Vaughan's Herbertian Poetic

JONATHAN NAUMAN

No instance of poetic discipleship under George Herbert has received more attention or commentary than Henry Vaughan's. Since the mid-nineteenth century revival of Vaughan's literary reputation, readers have tracked hundreds of verbal parallels between Vaughan's works and *The Temple*; and the movement in devotional verse that Herbert inspired[1] seems to have found its most quotable expression in the 1654 Preface to *Silex Scintillans*, where Vaughan honors 'the blessed man, Mr. *George Herbert*, whose holy *life* and *verse* gained many pious *Converts*, (of whom I am the least).'[2] Yet, readers of Vaughan and Herbert also predictably agree that when Vaughan succeeds as a poet, he does so in a literary vein quite distinct from Herbert's. I intend here to read three poems from Vaughan which emulate Herbert's 'holy *life* and *verse*' in three different ways, hoping in the process to clarify how Vaughan's distinctive visionary poetic can be considered Herbertian.

Vaughan's most explicit lyric response to *The Temple* can be found near the center of the first issue of *Silex Scintillans* in a poem called 'The Match' (191-192), whose first section is written in direct address to Herbert. Vaughan's editors have tracked in detail[3] this poem's verbal interactions with Herbert's 'Obedience,'[4] which lyric provides Vaughan's devotional starting point:

---

1 This movement, as Helen Wilcox has shown in '"Scribling under so faire a Coppy": the presence of Herbert in the poetry of Vaughan's contemporaries,' *Scintilla* 7 (2003), pp. 185-200, included both men and women poets, and comprised writers from a full range of political, theological, and educational backgrounds.

2 Alan Rudrum, ed., *Henry Vaughan: The Complete Poems* (Harmondsworth, Middlesex: Penguin Books, 1976 [1983]), p. 142. Quotations below from Vaughan are cited within my text from this edition.

3 See L. C. Martin, ed., *The Works of Henry Vaughan*, 2nd ed. (Oxford: Clarendon Press, 1957), p. 736; French Fogle, ed., *The Complete Poetry of Henry Vaughan* (New York: New York University Press, 1965), p. 190; Rudrum, pp. 559-60. Each of these editions has been helpful throughout this paper in tracking the textual links between Vaughan and Herbert.

4 Helen Wilcox, ed., *The English Poems of George Herbert* (Cambridge: Cambridge University Press, 2007), pp. 374-75. Quotations below from Herbert are cited within my text from this edition.

My God, if writings may
Convey a Lordship any way
Whither the buyer and the seller please;
Let it not thee displease
If this poore paper do as much as they.

On it my heart doth bleed
As many lines, as there doth need
To passe it self and all it hath to thee.
To which I do agree,
And here present it as my speciall deed.

If that hereafter Pleasure
Cavill, and claim her part and measure,
As if this passed with a reservation,
Or some such words in fashion;
I here exclude the wrangler from thy treasure.

* * *

He that will passe his land,
As I have mine, may set his hand
And heart unto this deed, when he hath read;
And make the purchase spread
To both our goods, if he to it will stand.

How happie were my part,
If some kinde man would thrust his heart
Into these lines; till in heav'ns court of rolls
They were by winged souls
Entred for both, farre above their desert! (ll. 1-5, 36-45).

So Herbert's lyric proposes; and Vaughan answers the invitation as follows:

Dear friend! Whose holy, ever-living lines
Have done much good
To many, and have checked my blood,
My fierce, wild blood that still heaves, and inclines,
But is still tamed
By those bright fires which thee inflamed;

Here I join hands, and thrust my stubborn heart
Into thy *deed*,
There from no *duties* to be freed,
And if hereafter *youth*, or *folly* thwart
And claim their share,
Here I renounce the poisonous ware (ll. 1-12).

It has often been suggested that Vaughan read Herbert so avidly that verbal borrowing from *The Temple* became for him an unconscious practice, resulting in 'Herbert's words and images [being] put to surprisingly different uses and applications.'[5] In 'The Match,' interaction with Herbert is fully conscious, but another form of literary nonintentionality seems to emerge even as Vaughan describes the process by which Herbert's verse has transformed his sensibility. Jonathan Post has especially noticed Vaughan's positioning of Herbert's 'lines' as mediators of God's 'bright fires,' an image that emanates from the triple pun of Vaughan's 'Match' title but which lacks any precedent in 'Obedience.'[6] Though other Herbertian texts may have helped to supply the image,[7] Vaughan's 'bright fires' depart from the tone and content of the lyric to which he is replying; and Herbert's soberly humorous parable likening Christian commitment to a real estate transaction becomes a recondite background detail for Vaughan's presentation of his master as a benevolent magus whose words of command continually subdue his follower's passions.

The relayed fire, moreover, is not the only noticeable innovation. When Herbert suggested that his reader might 'set his hand / And heart unto this deed' (ll. 37-38), it seems to me that he meant 'hand' and 'heart' to figure a written endorsement backed by honest intent. Vaughan's response, 'Here I join hands, and thrust my stubborn heart / Into thy *deed*' (ll. 7-8), supplies a rejoinder much more tactile and gregarious than Herbert's text seems to anticipate; and 'There from no *duties* to be freed' (l. 9) seems addressed, at least secondarily, to Herbert himself as God's intermediary. The tone is cavalier and Royalist: Vaughan joins hands with a fellow spiritual soldier; and one remembers a passage in Vaughan's lyric 'Abel's Blood' which seems to imply that Vaughan fulfilled a vow made to God amidst the stresses of battle when he dedicated his poetic talent entirely to sacred topics.[8]

5 Joseph E. Summers, *The Heirs of Donne and Jonson* (New York and London: Oxford University Press, 1970), p. 121; see also E. C. Pettet, *Of Paradise and Light: A Study of Vaughan's 'Silex Scintillans'* (Cambridge: Cambridge University Press), p. 61.

6 Jonathan Post, *Henry Vaughan: The Unfolding Vision* (Princeton, NJ: Princeton University Press, 1982), pp. 119-20.

7 I would suggest the 'fire-work' of Herbert's 'The Starre' (268, l. 9) and perhaps the apostolic fire of Herbert's 'Whitsunday' (213, l.5).

8 See 'Abel's Blood,' ll. 27-32 (291).

Perhaps even more important than the bright fires and joining of hands is Vaughan's initial reference to Herbert's verses as 'holy, ever-living lines' (l. 1). In 'Obedience,' Herbert presented his poem as his 'speciall deed,' requesting that his readers use his writing as a nonspecific contractual document, a written mediation functioning on analogy with the Protestant conception of Scripture enabling and transmitting salvific Christian knowledge. Vaughan, his Anglican emphases those of a Civil War era cavalier, tacitly moves beyond what Herbert's invitation strictly calls for by characterizing Herbert's verses as a continuation of Herbert's holy person. Such appreciation of Herbert's work anticipates the close connections Vaughan sees between authorial action and literary action in the 1654 Preface's denunciation of immoral verse:

> It is a sentence of sacred authority, that *he that is dead, is freed from sin*; because he cannot in that *state*, which is without the *body*, sin any more; but he that writes *idle books* makes for himself another *body*, in which he always *lives*, and *sins* (after *death*) as *fast* and as *foul*, as ever he did in his *life*; which very consideration, deserves to be a sufficient *antidote* against this evil disease (140).

The transition from the first part of 'The Match' to the second takes us from oath of fealty to active engagement: Vaughan turns to God, and addresses Him in Herbert's manner.[9] In multiple instances, the address is also in Herbert's phraseology. This is the mode of emulation that has garnered most notice from Vaughan's readers. One remembers the conclusion of Herbert's 'The Offering,'

> Yet thy favour
> May give savour
> To this poore oblation;
> And it raise
> To be thy praise,
> And be my salvation (510, ll. 37-42),

in Vaughan's first three lines,

> Accept, dread Lord, the poor oblation,
> It is but poor,
> Yet through thy mercies may be more (191, ll. 1-3)

9 Vaughan's practice of changing the addressed audience within a poem—from George Herbert to God in 'The Match'; from his own profane poems to his sacred verse in 'Joy' (254-255); from the reader to God (through the persona of the divinely-planted 'Seed'), to the 'seed' itself, and then back again to the reader in 'The Seed Growing Secretly' (276-78)—accentuates his authorial presence in his sacred verse and has little precedent in *The Temple*.

and Vaughan's emphatic repetition of 'poor' brings back the 'poore paper' of Herbert's 'Obedience' (l.5). And so Vaughan's prayer associatively proceeds: as Herbert made his surrender of self to God a real estate contract, Vaughan warrants his service to the Divinity in terms of another Herbertian metaphor for spiritual ownership,[10] a sequence of land tenancies (ll. 7-15). As Herbert made his 'Deed' obligatory rather than voluntary upon recalling the Passion of Christ, Vaughan seals his request for total self-dedication with a reference to the Passion (ll. 16-21) in words borrowed from Herbert's 'Longing' (514, ll. 31-34).

'The Match' seems to inaugurate a consciously arranged Herbertian heart for *Silex Scintillans* Part One. The exact center of that volume is occupied by the very next poem, 'Rules and Lessons' (192-196), whose form and tenor emulate Herbert's 'The Church-porch' (6-24): the longest sacred lyric Vaughan ever published, it provides twenty-four stanzas of '*ordinary Instructions for a regular life*.'[11] 'Holy Scriptures' (197-198) follows almost immediately, an emulation of Herbert's double sonnet of the same title (58).

Welcome dear book, soul's joy, and food! The feast
    Of spirits, heaven extracted lies in thee;
    Thou art life's charter, the Dove's spotless nest
Where souls are hatched unto Eternity.

In thee the hidden stone, the *Manna* lies,
    Thou art the great *Elixir*, rare, and choice;
    The key that opens to all mysteries,
The *Word* in Characters, God in the *voice*.

O that I had deep cut in my hard heart
    Each line in thee! Then would I plead in groans
    Of my Lord's penning, and by sweetest art
Return upon himself the *Law*, and *Stones*.
    Read here, my faults are thine. This Book, and I
    Will tell thee so; *Sweet Saviour thou didst die!*

A reader knowledgeable of both Herbert's works and Vaughan's might be inclined to term this lyric a devotional pastiche rather than a literary emulation. The first two lines encapsulate the octet of Herbert's 'The H. Scriptures [I]' (208), lines three and four the first stanza of Herbert's 'Whitsunday' (213). The

10 'Love unknown' (453, ll. 3-5).

11 Martin, p. 140.

'hidden stone' of line five seems to fetch up its own Herbertian source in line six with the word '*Elixir*.' And certainly it is the stony heart of Herbert's 'The Altar' (92) that longs for the 'Lord's penning' in lines nine through eleven. One remembers the 'Exalted Manna' and 'Reversed thunder' of Herbert's 'Prayer [I]' (178) in lines five and twelve, and the 'Testament' thrust into God's hand in Herbert's 'Judgement' (654) with the words of line thirteen, 'my faults are thine.' Vaughan wrote for an audience already familiar with *The Temple*, and must therefore have allowed for his reader's experience of 'Holy Scriptures' to include this sequence of Herbertian hieroglyphics. Although E. C. Pettet has shown that Vaughan's borrowings do sometimes lend a dramatic 'force and richness' lacking in his originals,[12] the allusions here seem to scatter and dull the impact of Vaughan's poem, since almost every one of the appropriated images is integral to a separate poem in *The Temple* and better developed there.

On the other hand, I don't find myself able to join those readers who dismiss Vaughan's 'Holy Scriptures' as a bad poem.[13] Though not a particularly memorable work, it is a straightforward and competent metaphysical assemblage; and the foregrounding of hermetic and apocalyptic imagery makes the sonnet identifiably Vaughan's. One also notes the speaker's ambition in the poem's conclusion to personally become the Bible, a sentiment for which I don't know any antecedent in Herbert's work. The Scriptures are not assimilated in Herbert's verse. They assimilate. The Bible 'pennes and sets us down';[14] its 'holy leaves' are the echo of bliss;[15] its 'words do find me out.'[16] Although Vaughan testified similarly to the Bible's active agency,[17] he was a man of the Anglican Counter-Reformation's second phase,[18] for whom *sola Scriptura* had come to seem vulnerable to exploitation as a rationale for insurrection and religious chaos; furthermore, his imagination had been seized by a love for the mediating personal sanctities of figures such as Dionysius the Areopagite, Paulinus and Therasia

12 Pettet, p. 68.

13 One such reader includes 'Holy Scriptures' in a list of six poems from *Silex Scintillans* that she finds 'disconcertingly trite and sententious, even banal'; see Margaret Willy, *Three Metaphysical Poets* (London: Longmans, Green, and Co., 1961), p. 27.

14 'The bunch of grapes' (449, l. 11).

15 'Heaven' (656, ll. 11-12).

16 'The H. Scriptures (II)' (210, l. 11).

17 See Vaughan's autobiographical account of the Scriptures' role in his return to serious religious observance in 'To the Holy Bible' (310-11).

18 Graham Parry recounts the progress and artistic manifestations of this movement, distinguishing the moderate first phase, inspired by the living example of Lancelot Andrewes and the writings of Richard Hooker, from the second and more aggressive phase under William Laud. See especially his summary analysis of George Herbert's career as epitomizing the movement's moderate first phase in *Glory, Laud and Honour: The Arts of the Anglican Counter-Reformation* (Woodbridge, Suffolk: The Boydell Press, 2006), pp. 132-40.

of Nola, Anselm of Canterbury. His new poetic ambition was to testify with these early saints to experienced holiness, and to the sacred longings and visionary glimpses into eternity that such holiness enabled. George Herbert thus became for him a recent example of this salvific patristic holiness, a hierarch to be paired with Hierotheus, the teacher of the mystic Areopagite.

A number of Vaughan's readers have noticed that verbal echoes of George Herbert decrease as one passes from the first book of *Silex Scintillans* to the second. Some critics with romantic sympathies have seen in this a salutary waning of Herbert's influence over a younger 'poet who had much of his own to say.'[19] Some critics with modernist sympathies have considered it as evidence of poetic decline, suggesting that Vaughan had begun to evade the discipline of Herbertian stanza in favor of the 'conventional couplet-rhetoric' of his early Jonsonian verse.[20] However, these analyses would not seem to account for the fact that Vaughan's most adulatory prose references to George Herbert belong to the years during which the second edition of *Silex Scintillans* was being composed. 'Man in Darkness,' Vaughan's extended devotional meditation in *The Mount of Olives* (1652), quotes Herbert's lyric 'Life' (341) in full, as the work of 'a most glorious true *Saint* and a *Seer*'[21]; the reader's introduction to *Flores Solitudinis* (1654) quotes two stanzas of Herbert's lyric 'Content' (250) as a paradigm of that honorable 'temper *which can lay* by *the* garland, *when he may keepe it* on'[22]; and, as we have seen, few tributes to Herbert exceed what Vaughan offered in the Preface to the second edition of *Silex Scintillans* (1655). On a purely verbal level, it may be correct to say with E. C. Pettet that Vaughan's use of Herbert lessened as the 1650s went on, and that 'the finest of Vaughan's poems . . . are on the whole the ones in which Herbert's presence is least felt.'[23] But I think it fairly evident that in 1655 Vaughan himself would have strongly rejected any suggestion that his verses were owing less and less to George Herbert. The change had come rather, Vaughan would have said, from drawing closer to Herbert in spirit, from pursuing Herbert's vision to the point of neglecting mere stylistic imitation.

Vaughan's peculiar excellence as a poet owes much to his ability to present the philosophical insights of Christian Platonism and hermetism as experienced states of mind; and one often finds that his most intense lyrics of sacred longing verbally quote or closely paraphrase his devotional readings and translations:

19 Pettet, p. 65.

20 Louis Martz, *The Paradise Within: Studies in Vaughan, Traherne, and Milton* (New Haven and London: Yale University Press, 1964), p. 4.

21 Martin, p. 186.

22 Martin, p. 216.

23 Pettet, p. 67.

But felt through all this fleshly dress
Bright *shoots* of everlastingness:[24]

this bit of 'couplet-rhetoric' comes almost verbatim from Owen Felltham[25];

O Father of eternal life, and all
Created glories under thee!
Resume thy spirit from this world of thrall
Into true liberty:[26]

this comes, just as closely, from the Egyptian Camephes, by way of the Jesuit John Nieremberg.[27] Tetrameter couplets and ample stanza forms often seem to enable intense renderings or dramatizations of thoughts from Vaughan's devotional writings or readings; and when Vaughan succeeds with complex stanza forms, as in 'The World' (227-228) or 'The Morning-Watch' (179), the forms do not contribute a splendid seamlessness of statement as is generally the case in *The Temple*; rather, they lend musical counterpoint to a voice of vatic poise and authority. It is the same voice that we hear in the manifesto of the 1654 Preface when Vaughan subordinates sacred poetic excellence to devotional discipline and then identifies the implementation of that order of priorities as the only real way to emulate George Herbert.

> It is true indeed, that to give up our thoughts to pious *themes* and *contemplations* (if it be done for piety's sake) is a great *step* towards *perfection*; because it will *refine*, and *dispose* to devotion and sanctity. And further, it will *procure* for us (so easily communicable is that *loving spirit*) some small *prelibation* of those heavenly *refreshments*, which descend but seldom, and then very sparingly, upon *men* of ordinary or indifferent *holiness*; but he that desires to excel in this kinde of *hagiography*, or holy writing, must strive (by all means) for *perfection* and true *holiness*, that a *door may be opened for him in heaven*, Rev. iv 1 and then he will be able to write (with *Hierotheus* and holy *Herbert*) A *true hymn* (142).

24 'The Retreat' (173, ll. 19-20).

25 Martin, p. 733.

26 'They are all gone into the world of light!' (247, ll. 33-36).

27 Martin, p. 284. For more detailed reviews of the connections between Vaughan's devotional translations and *Silex Scintillans*, see my articles on 'Nieremberg's Patience of the Saints: Experiencing *Flores Solitudinis* in *Silex Scintillans*,' *Scintilla* 13 (2009), pp. 160-74 and 'Alternative Saints: Eucherius, Paulinus of Nola, and Henry Vaughan's *Silex Scintillans*,' *The Seventeenth Century* 26, ii (Autumn 2011), pp. 264-78.

Here is a straightforward statement of Henry Vaughan's Herbertian poetic, his platonic participatory understanding of Herbert's common-sense maxim,

> The finenesse which a hymne or psalme affords,
> Is, when the soul unto the lines accords.[28]

Vaughan simultaneously communicates and demonstrates this sacred poetic near the end of the second issue of *Silex Scintillans* in a lyric of contemplative rapture called 'The Query' (309):

> O tell me whence that joy doth spring,
> Whose diet is divine and fair,
> Which wears heaven, like a bridal ring,
> And tramples on doubts and despair?
>
> Whose eastern traffic deals in bright
> And boundless empyrean themes,
> Mountains of spice, day-stars and light,
> Green trees of life, and living streams?
>
> Tell me, O tell who did thee bring
> And here, without my knowledge, placed,
> Till thou didst grow and get a wing,
> A wing with eyes, and eyes that taste?
>
> Sure, *holiness* the *magnet* is,
> And *love* the *lure*, that woos thee down;
> Which makes the high transcendent bliss
> Of knowing thee, so rarely known.

Here we have, essentially, an ecstatic lyrical rendition of Vaughan's claims about the origins of true sacred verse. Although the poem, so far as I have been able to track, is free of verbal borrowings from *The Temple*, it clearly means to provide the '*prelibation*' of 'heavenly *refreshments*' that Vaughan attributes to '*Hierotheus* and holy *Herbert*' in the Preface. It is perhaps Vaughan's 'true Hymne,' delivered not in the manner of Herbert's open parsonly colloquy on 'My joy, my life, my crown,' but as an overheard meditation in which Vaughan identifies his own sacred muse as a 'seed' of the Holy Spirit.[29]

28 'A true Hymne' (576, ll. 9-10).

29 The '*magnet*' of l. 13 recalls once again Vaughan's interest in the hermetic sciences, and connects this poem with the 'magnetism' and 'sunny seed' of the rooster in 'Cock-Crowing' (251).

Certainly this poem epitomizes Vaughan's peculiar talent, its tone and content of the very sort readers cite when they contrast Vaughan with Herbert. The Scriptural allusions generally add an apocalyptic note, especially appropriate as Vaughan's collection approaches its end: the mystic Bride of the Lamb 'descending out of heaven from God' (Rev. 22: 9-10); the plea for the returning Christ to make haste 'upon the mountains of spices' (Cant. 8: 14);[30] the 'day star' of the eschaton to be awaited within the light of inspired prophecy (II Pet. 1: 19); the river of life flowing from the throne of God and the tree whose leaves 'were for the healing of the nations' (Rev. 22: 1-2); the worshipping beasts winged with eyes (Rev. 4: 8); the ability of those delivered by the Angel of the Lord to 'taste and see that the Lord is good' (Ps. 34: 7-8). As Frank Kermode and John Hollander once put it, 'even the biblical allusions are strongly colored by the strange and strong imagination that brings them together.'[31] And as the allusions build and unfold, Vaughan credits this imaginative progression to a divine inspiration 'here, without my knowledge, placed.' One feels that a door has indeed opened in heaven, to reveal a voice calling for one to 'Come up hither!' (Rev. 4: 1), that God's falconry has struck the '*lure*' and brought one in Vaughan's company to a rare experience of 'the high transcendent bliss / Of knowing' God. One also suspects that Vaughan would not deny that the '*love*' of his falcon-lure included three lyrics of that name by the poet of whose converts he was the least.

30 Influential Protestant commentators took *Canticles* to be an apocalyptic pastoral; see William Tate, *Solomonic Iconography in Early Stuart England* (Lampeter, Ceredigion: Edwin Mellen, 2001), pp. 241-42.

31 See *The Literature of Renaissance England* (New York: Oxford University Press, 1973), p. 690. It's surely also relevant to mention that Vaughan's first language was Welsh, and to remember the letter he wrote John Aubrey about the Welsh shepherd who became a gifted bard following a vision of being struck by a hawk (Martin, p. 696).

'Spiced Wine' by Tanja Butler.

MARIA APICHELLA

An Epileptic Entering Chartres Cathedral

Out of squinted shapeless
blocks of yellow into big musty blue.
Cold   laced air singing tingling
– étoiles ciel – window splashes watery
wine, chunks of softened-sun butter,
bruised blue squares, flicker on skin & stone.
Hot clover drifts transparent
thick in throat & temples.

Inside the crypt flame petals, white.
Cyclamen flowers gigantic
in a bowl of darkness.
the petals divide,
moving apart like hands after prayers
transform
from foliage to faces.
Shadowed nuns
hidden by headdress
whisper, fade.

Star-lit

road, narrow and glazed
with old icy snow.

The long lights
sliced the night.

Outside the Milky Way
swirled and was still.

We stopped
scrambled out the car

stood, breathing.

NICHOLAS MURRAY

Diptych

That's you,
wind-ruffled
on the rear deck,
seabirds in pursuit,
the wake like a spreading tail.

That's me,
ignoring you,
jabbing my finger at the sleek
slip and leap of dolphin,
my stomach hard against the salt-rough rail.

The Empty Book

An Empty Book is like an Infant's Soul, in which any thing may be Written.
It is Capable of all Things, but containeth Nothing.
I have a Mind to fill this with Profitable Wonders.

Thomas Traherne

It is a white space
where any act of love
may be performed;

where primped pillows,
and starched sheets,
wait to be disordered.

Here is making,
shape-shifting
word-working;

here is spoor of print,
the marks that tell
of something live

that has crossed
the empty space
leaving its trace

like the thin coil
of the sand-worm
on a hard beach

where waves recede
disinclined to wipe
the fresh inscription.

ROGER GARFITT

After the Great Storm

Wind shear tore sleep away with the tiles.
Looked out at the parking lot
– it had turned back into Paradise.

But the car was still there, long shadow
under the handstand of a pine branch.
Get to London or lose a day's work!

Strange how regular the shockwaves were,
the trees along the coast road reduced
to a pattern in flock wallpaper.

Still in the twentieth century,
an overrider in his sealed pod,
I turned onto the A23

and found myself back in the greenwood,
shadow where the carriageway had been
and the ridged bark of a fallen tree.

Then a shine to my right, two tyre tracks
of flattened grass . . . someone had slipped
over the central reservation,

as if instinct had been there all along,
only awaiting its chance to awake.
I drove against an absence of traffic,

the morning light still quick on creatures
out of their element, their windward twigs
chamfered to a millimetric gleam,

so alive had they been to the air.
One by one, I passed them, a gnat's whine
through their stillness, and came on a trunk

there was no passing, its snapped-off roots
high overhead, and a policeman
scaled down to a manikin waving me

round the back of it, the carriageway down
to a forest path and the tyres pressing
as though theirs were the first footfall.

ALYSON HALLETT

The Last Time

The last time I saw him
he refused to speak.
Arms folded
he stared into the middle
distance, looked through me
as if I was made of glass.
We were in a white marquee –
people milled around
buying paintings, pottery,
bespoke tables and chairs.
Why won't you talk to me
I yelled: it was a weird way
for five years of loving to end.
I staggered out through
an open flap into a furnace
of light. I couldn't breathe.
There were people smiling
and drinking Pimms,
ice-cubes, slices of cucumber
and strawberry knocking
against tumbler walls,
faint tang of mint.
The tall, evergreen pines
saw me stumble
into an orchard and collapse,
hands and knees in the dirt,
like a dog, the earth mercifully
hard beneath me.

MATTHEW BARTON

Walking the Frome

By Snuff Mills you're extinguished
to slug brown, girding your loin
for the cover-up coming, the decline
below tarmac, slow trudge
through the gut of the city.

But you flicker into life as I follow you out
past Frenchay and under the shudder
of a ring road through bramble and copse, across fields:
not quite singing but starting to whisper
of things once being livelier –

weary of the future but as yet
not oblivious of beginnings. Round bends
you show flare on occasion and willing
not to think yet of culverts
far off still but waiting

to siphon and swallow you. There's a lilt
in your swift lack of umbrage, your eagerness
to rush towards what's round the corner,
though some might detect subtle darkening
of mood in your chatter.

Near Frampton Cotterell you're humming
in the mouths of stone bridges,
shrugging your way past old workings
at Iron Acton and cutting your losses
in fields where you might be mistaken

for glorified ditches. You keep flowing,
at moments a leash quivering on
the tug of bad portents, at others
remembering the spring you unspool from
you let down your hair in a clear
torrent of abandon.

It's at Yate though when you've been yet again
artificially channelled and straitened
and are clogged up with tatters of plastic,
rusty tins and thick gunk
that you're suddenly emblazoned
in a white heron sailing serene
from your tongue like the soul
having done with it all and ascending.

PHILIP GROSS

Spiegel im Spiegel

Three variations on a theme by Arvo Pärt

1.
All that is, or ever
needs be said,
                    contained
in frame reflecting frame
containing
                all that is and
its companion: is that one
or two
 eternities?

2.
The narrow path the music walks on
round its cloister, never turning yet
returns
          in a Möbius way, an Escher,
on the underside-now-up of the world,
its surface:
               what became of gravity?

3.
That kind of love: as if they had met,
approaching down a corridor with no
two ways about it, only to the pole,

the fixed point, of their meeting: as if one
step closer and they'll pass into,
or through, each other,

into nowhere
anyone
can be.

At the back of the mirror

there's no other room
unless it's this:
                    its patch of ingrained
shadow on the wall, damp maybe,
          maybe mould,
          when it's gone.

Or stranger, the bright-print
of unfashionable-now
                              cerise,
a new chemical yellow, a lettucy green,
          on paper faded else-
          where in the sunlight,

elsewhen: not unlike that other
room, in fact,
                    of stories, watching you
as if you were their skewed reflection,
          from the corner of, yet out
          of reach of, time.

The mirror that the moon was caught in

breaks. Is that the bad luck broken too?

Or doubled? Or spreading out, into no longer
countable winks and splinters:

you can sweep and wipe and pick your way for ever;
there's always be one
you don't find until it finds you.

A prayer

for mirrors, then,
for their particular distress:

to be come to, as if you had promised to be
a window, opening

onto a room in which the looker is their better self
– hard not to take the blame

for all that disappointment, or
to feel the wingbeats,
panic-flutter at the pane, to get in, to get out,
of conceit or self hate

– how all this wears away
your silver: feel the tarnish spreading, age
spots in your vision,
lapses

– yes, distress

that no huff of the lips, just close enough
to warm you, no curt wipe of the cuff
can correct:

a prayer, then,
for them, severally alone –

for those who should not pray together
though they're so one family, so
almost one

in station washroom or boutique hotel en-suite
or dosshouse: loneliness

of those who have the world to share, and must
not meet, not face to face
on pain of infinite regress.

The insatiable benevolence

of mirrors: to give everything back.
To keep nothing, almost nothing

for themselves. A fleck of dust
maybe. A skin-flake. What can you do

except feed them and feed them
yourself? Without hope. It is a marriage

made not quite in heaven but its mirror
image. Flawless, selfless, the ministering

angels. It could make you long for hell.

Set design for the interior opera

after the installation Untitled (2013)
by Kristiina Harsen & Johannes Süre

: a light-box
in a dark room
lined with mirrors
: an infinite lawn

extends in squares,
into cubes of itself,
itself to the power
of *x*, into gradually

more nuanced shadow,
gradations of the not-
quite-sound that's not
the hiss of sprinklers,

not the wind . . . more
like the after-image
of a human breath –
love-gasp or final ex

-piration: stepping stones
that lead in all directions
into almost-darkness,
hush, with black

drapes soon to shudder
and part, through which
a figure, very small
at first, for whom

we have no name
or costume, might step
out, onto the stage
      and sing.

Enough,

turn my face to the wall.

Or no. No,

even darkness
has a mirror image

if we just had eyes to see.

David Jones, Metaphysical Poet

JEREMY HOOKER

David Jones's principal reference to the Metaphysical poets of the seventeenth century occurs in a footnote to Preface to *The Anathemata*. He appends the note to a passage concerning what he and his Catholic friends – the intellectuals of the Chelsea Group – called 'The Break'. This 'had reference to something which was affecting the entire world of sacrament and sign'.

> Water is called the 'matter' of the Sacrament of Baptism. Is 'two of hydrogen and one of oxygen that "matter"'? I suppose so. But what concerns us here is whether the poet can and does so juxtapose and condition within a context the formula H_2O as to evoke 'founts', 'that innocent creature', 'the womb of this devine font', 'the candidates', or for that matter 'the narrows' and the siluer sea, Which serves it in the office of a wall, Or as a Moat defensiue to a house'.

He proceeds to say that 'knowledge of the chemical composition of this material water should, normally,' deepen the significance of 'the sacrament of water', and also the significance of our British *materia poetica*, of which water is very much a part. He then asks us to 'consider how the men of some epochs have managed to wed widely separated ideas, and to make odd scraps of newly discovered data subserve immemorial themes'. He offers 'the English Metaphysicals' as an example of poets who have managed this wedding of novelty and tradition.

Jones's note on 'the English Metaphysics' reads in part as follows:

> Who wrote a poetry that was counter-Renaissant, creaturely yet other-world-ordered, ecstatical yet technically severe and ingenious, concerned with conditions of the psyche, but its images very much of the soma; metaphysical, but not un-intrigued by the physics of the period; English, but well represented by names hardly English.[1]

---

1 David Joes, *The Anathemata* (London: Faber and Faber, 1952), pp. 16-17. Further quotations from *The Anathemata* will be from this edition, referenced *A* in the text.

For Jones and his Catholic friends, it was not the validity of religion that 'The Break' called into question. David Jones was not a poet of religious doubt. His life and work were founded upon the conviction that art 'deals with realities and the real is sacred and religious'.[2] The problem for a sacramental poet in an age dominated by secular and utilitarian values was the validity of his language and his images. Sacramental language, as the passage above testifies, is profoundly evocative. It has recession and depth; it calls up the things that belong not only to a culture, but also to the divine Creation. But can a poet use scientific data such as a chemical formula to serve as a sacramental image?

It was the war in which he had fought that initially made this question so urgent for David Jones. As he wrote in Preface to *In Parenthesis*:

> We who are of the same world of sense with hairy ass and furry wolf and who presume to other and more radiant affinities, are finding it difficult, as yet, to recognise these creatures of chemicals as true extensions of ourselves, that we may feel for them a native affection, which alone can make them magical for us.[3]

'Creature' and 'magical' are keywords in Jones's conception of the Creation. The question concerning language's signifying power involves recognition of kinship and fellow feeling with non-human creatures. It is fundamentally a question of love.

Faced with this question, Jones, in the words quoted above, asks us 'to consider how the men of some epochs have managed to wed widely separated ideas, and to make odd scraps of newly discovered data subserve immemorial themes'. He perceives 'the English Metaphysicals' as such men. In this view, the Metaphysical poets of the seventeenth century adopted the new sciences into their enchanted world-view, instead of finding them agents of disenchantment.

Jones's reference to wedding 'widely separated ideas' contrasts radically with Samuel Johnson's allegation in his 'Life of Cowley' that, in Metaphysical poetry: 'The most heterogeneous ideas are yoked by violence together'. Jones does not see this poetry as a break from tradition, but rather as an adaptation of new ideas to immemorial themes. Clearly he is not thinking of John Donne's reaction to New Philosophy casting all in doubt or of what Marjorie Hope Nicolson called 'the breaking of the circle'.[4] In noting what he sees in English Meta-

2 David Jones, *Epoch and Artist* (London: Faber and Faber 1959), p. 158. Further quotations from *Epoch and Artist* will be from this edition, referenced *E & A* in the text.

3 David Jones, *In Parenthesis*, Faber and Faber (1937), new edition (London, 1963), p. xiv. Further quotations from *In Parenthesis* will be from this edition, referenced *IP* in the text.

4 The references are to John Donne's 'The First Anniversary' and Marjorie Hope Nicolson's *The Breaking of the Circle* (New York: Columbia University Press, 1960).

physical poetry, especially in referring to it as 'counter-Renaissant, creaturely yet other-world-ordered', with 'images very much of the soma', Jones might also have been summing up what he sought to achieve as a Christian poet in the modern world.

In describing the Metaphysicals Jones may have had in mind the Donne of T. S. Eliot's famous essay, 'The Metaphysical Poets', a poet who felt 'thought as immediately as the odour of a rose'.[5] Feeling thought is very different from the idea of the Metaphysical poets that descends from Dryden and Johnson, and it may be contrasted with the most damaging thing Johnson said about them: that they wrote 'rather as beholders than partakers of human nature'. Truer by far to the life-world of the Metaphysical poets are the words from Acts xvii, 27-28 that Henry Vaughan appends to 'The Search': 'That they should seek the Lord, if happily they might feel after him, and find him, though he be not far off from every one of us, for in him we live, and move, and have our being'.[6]

Jones notes that the poetry of the Metaphysical poets was 'concerned with conditions of the psyche, but it was very much of the soma'. This accords with his belief 'that all good poetry must hold up a clear bodily image & that the work is done by that image – so that the general shines out from the particular'.[7] Feeling their thought, the Metaphysical poets wrote poetry of the whole human being, not of a disembodied mind. They were poets who responded body and soul to the Incarnation.

Rather than beholders of life, Metaphysical poets were 'partakers of human nature'. This was as true, or truer, of Donne's poems addressed to God as it was of his poems teasing or cajoling or solacing a lover. George Herbert's religious poems are poems of devotion to God, in which he humbly expresses a personal relationship with Christ. Consider this line from 'The Elixer':

> 'All may of thee partake'

Helen Wilcox glosses 'partake' as 'share, take a part' and says: 'The primary meaning is eucharistic'.[8] This is true of David Jones's art, as well. Already, in *In Parenthesis*, we glimpse the sacrifice re-enacted in the Mass as the all-encompassing reality. The emphasis falls upon *all*. Stanley Spencer said of a work of

5 *Selected Prose of T. S. Eliot*, ed. by Frank Kermode (London: Faber and Faber, 1975), p. 64.

6 Henry Vaughan, *The Complete Poems*, ed. by Alan Rudrum (Harmondsworth: Penguin Books, 1983), p. 159.

7 Quoted in Thomas Dilworth, *David Jones Engraver, Soldier, Painter, Poet* (London: Jonathan Cape, 2017), p. 124.

8 *The English Poems of George Herbert*, ed. by Helen Wilcox (Cambridge: Cambridge University Press, 2007), p. 642.

art, 'All must be safely gathered in' (*E & A*, p. 243). For Jones, this was true of the Mass, which, Saunders Lewis said, '*makes sense* of everything'.[9]

Preface to *In Parenthesis* begins:

> This writing has to do with some things I saw, felt, & was part of. (*IP*, p. ix)

The work that follows is notable for its immediacy. We partake with John Ball, who is a figure for the poet, of events that he and his comrades were part of. At the same time, *In Parenthesis* is 'a shape in words', a work of art informed by the feelings and thought of a man with a fully developed philosophy of human nature. Later, he would write: 'man is a "borderer", he is the sole inhabitant of a tract of country where matter marches with spirit, so that whatever he does, good or bad, affects the economy of these two domains'. (*E&A*, p. 86) The image recurs when he speaks of: 'marshes, which are also marches, the march-lands of matter and spirit, time and not time.' (*E&A*, p. 202)

The trenches, which are depicted realistically in *In Parenthesis*, are also symbolic 'march-lands of matter and spirit, time and not-time'. In the imagery and allusions time is porous and opens upon a timeless pattern. The material landscape is otherworldly. In terrible conditions the poem offers a vision of goodness in the care that the men show one another, and in allusions to 'the Lord of Order', the figure of Arthur that represents a type of Christ.[10]

The trenches constitute a world in which the men share conditions in common with other creatures, animals, but also trees and the elements, and in which they are made to experience their being as creatures. 'Creaturely', the word Jones applied to the Metaphysical poets, is central to his apprehension of life. Robin Ironside may have been the first to write about Jones's Franciscan sensibility.[11] Jones's Franciscan sympathies were present from the first, in boyhood drawings of a bear, and a wolf and other creatures. His Franciscan sense of shared creatureliness is fundamental to his poetry and paintings. It is a feeling for creatures, and feeling informing words, as we see in his rendering of the rat of no-man's-land. The night sentry's meditation-cum-reverie as he listens to the rat places the war in a metaphysical context:

> You can hear the silence of it:
> you can hear the rat of no-man's-land

9 'Saunders Lewis introduces Two Letters from David Jones', *Mabon* 1, 5 (1972), p. 18.

10 'Arthur the Protector of the Land, the Leader, the Saviour, the Lord of Order carrying a aid into the place of Chaos' (*IP*, p. 201).

11 Robin Ironside, *David Jones*, The Penguin Modern Painters (Harmondsworth: Penguin ooks, 1949), p. 15.

rut-out intricacies,
weasel-out his patient workings,
scrut, scrut, sscrut,
harrow-out earthly, trowel his cunning paw;
redeem the time of our uncharity, to sap his own amphibious paradise.
(*IP*, p. 54)

Jones makes ironic use of Darwin's evolutionary theory as he proceeds to depict a process of devolution, in which noble creatures emblematic of battles in the past, 'the white-tailed eagle' of the Battle of Brunanburh, and 'the speckled kite of Maldon',

have naturally selected to be un-winged;
to go on the belly, to
sap sap sap
with festered spines, arched under the moon; furrit with
whiskered snouts the secret parts of us. (*IP*, p. 54)

Jones was not primarily an ironist, and the irony shown here coincides with sympathy shown for the rat, perceived as a fellow creature. The rat is likened to the men by use of language that belongs also to their activities, such as 'you can hear his carrying-parties rustle our corruptions', where 'corruptions' has moral force, as well as referring literally to human corpses. There is horror in the implication of rats feeding on dead men, but horror is subsumed by a sense of affinity. The rat is given its own point of view, its own purpose in the scheme of things, and the sounds it makes – 'scrut, scrut, sscrut' – give it its own 'voice'. It is present alongside the men with its own somatic qualities: 'bead-eyed', furriting 'with whiskered snout'. 'The rat of no-man's land' is at once a fellow creature and a creature with its own mode of being.

The success of *In Parenthesis* owes much to the way in which the narrator both takes part in the action and sees it in perspective. This is especially noticeable in Part 7 which deals with the most chaotic experience, the attack on Mametz Wood. Here, what the men feel is rendered from the inside in all its feverish terror. Within the same movement their felt extremity is juxtaposed with an external view:

you have not capacity for added fear only the limbs are leaden to negotiate the slope and rifles all out of balance, clumsied with long auxiliary steel
seem five times the regulation weight –

it bitches the aim as well;
                    and we ourselves as those small
cherubs, who trail awkwardly the weapons of the God in
                                        Fine Art Works. (*IP*, p. 156)

We might think of this as a cinematic technique that cuts between close up and panorama. The sudden widenings of perspective, the views from above, occur within a drama that is close to earth, in which men live like troglodytes and are akin to 'creatures of chalk', physically 'close with the mole/ in down and silky rodent,/ and if you look more intimately all manner of small creatures'. As the rats benefit from the soldiers' 'corruptions', so

created-dear things creep about quite comfortably
yet who travail until now
beneath your tin-hat shade. (*IP*, p. 157)

Enabling us to 'look more intimately' is what David Jones does in his poetry and painting. If we pause to ask what 'created-dear' means, we may see that it shows both God's love of his Creation and the human being's capacity for fellow feeling with all creatures.

The Franciscan spirit of 'tenderness for nature'[12] links David Jones with Metaphysical poets, their 'names hardly English'. He was given to theorizing about 'a Celtic tradition in English literature', which included 'a certain affection for the intimate creatureliness of things'. He found this in 'early medieval works' and emerging again 'with Shakespeare and the Metaphysical poets'.[13] We may relate his idea of this tradition to the Franciscan spirit, which, as E.A. Armstrong has pointed out, has affinities with the early mythology and poetry of the Irish and Welsh and is a strand within the history of Christian thinking. Among the seventeenth-century poets 'creaturely yet other-world-ordered' applies especially to the poets with the keenest sense of the natural world, to Henry Vaughan in poems such as 'The Morning Watch' and 'Rules and Lessons', to Herbert and Marvell with their love of flowers and fruits, and to Thomas Traherne, for whom the new sciences of astronomy and microscopy enhanced his sense of the wonder of the universe. There is no sentimentality in the poets' vision of the created world as a community of human and non-human beings. Francis called 'dumb animals, however small, *brother* and *sister*'. Finally, he welcomed 'Sister Death'.

12 Edward A. Armstrong, *Saint Francis: Nature Mystic* (Berkeley: University of California Press, 1976), p. 240.

13 Quoted in Dilworth, *David Jones: Engraver, Soldier, Painter, Poet*, p. 181.

The same figure appears in Mametz Wood:

> But sweet sister death has gone debauched today and stalks on the high ground with strumpet confidence, makes no coy veiling of her appetite but leers from you to me with all her parts discovered. (*IP*, p. 162)

This is ironic, but the bitterness does not annul the fact that in Jones's world death is 'sister', kin to the whole man, body and soul.

In the midst of the battle of Mametz Wood Private Ball asks the question to which all Jones's writings are an implicit answer:

> But why is Father Larkin talking to the dead? (*IP*, p. 173)

Shadowed in *In Parenthesis*, the underlying form of David Jones's subsequent writings is that of a Requiem Mass. It is a form combining prayer, commemoration and celebration that emerges with beautiful clarity in the prayer of the Priest of the Household in 'The Sleeping Lord':

> for the departed
> of the entire universal orbis
> from the unknown beginnings
> unguessed millenniums back
> until now:
> FOR THESE ALL
> he makes his silent, secret
> devout and swift memento.
> And discreetly and with scarcely any discernible movement
> he makes once again the salvific sign, saying less than half-
> audibly: *Requiem aeternum dona eis, Domine.*[14]

The Priest recalls Celtic Saints ('Athletes of God') 'in the habitat of wolves and wild-cat and such like creatures of the Logos (by whom all creatures are that are}' (*SL*, p. 79). In Jones's theology the Redemption is as inclusive as the Creation. The inclusiveness is symbolized by the ship and voyage imagery of *The Anathemata*, in which, invoking the authority of St Paul, Jones says: 'the argosy or voyage of the Redeemer . . . is offered to the Trinity . . . on behalf of us Argonauts and of the whole argosy of mankind, and, in some sense, of all sentient being and, perhaps, of insentient too'. (*A*, p. 106)

14 David Jones, *The Sleeping Lord and Other Fragments* (London: Faber and Faber, 1974), p. 86. Further quotations from *The Sleeping Lord* will be from this edition, referenced *SL* in the text.

David Jones was a writer and artist with a comprehensive theology who sought to make images of the whole. How his extraordinary mind worked may be seen in a passage from *The Dying Gaul*:

> Cézanne . . . said we must 'do Poussin again after nature'. Perhaps we might almost say that we must do Cézanne's apples again, after the nature of Julian of Norwich's little nut, which 'endureth and ever shall for God loveth it'.[15]

The reference is to Julian of Norwich's showing in which God showed Julian 'a little thing, the size of a hazelnut' and tells her: 'It is all that is made'.[16] Julian sees three truths in this image of the Creation: that God made it, and loves it, and sustains it. This vision of the Creation is Jones's vision too. He apprehended it, however, as a modern artist, in a post-impressionist world pioneered by Cézanne, and his task was to find modern means to express the vision. And here he came up against the problem of the mechanistic world-view that the Metaphysical poets of the seventeenth century had been able to side step.

Abstract formulae effectively denied the existence of the image-world on which his vision depended. It was in modern earth and life sciences that he found signs for creature and the Creation. Geology in particular excited his imagination. His response to it was quite different from Ruskin's, whose religious belief was unsettled by the geologists.[17] Ruskin and the Pre-Raphaelites influenced Jones's attention to detail. What he had and they lacked was a sense of God's energy and the linguistic means to express it. In a magnificent passage in 'The Sleeping Lord' culminating in 'the Word is made fire' (SL, p. 72) Jones renders the geological making of South Wales; and in *The Anathemata* he draws on life sciences to show the presence of 'the New Light' 'brighting' the entire material creation and biosphere 'from before all time':

> Piercing the eskered silt, discovering every stria, each score and macula,
> lighting all the fragile laminae of the shales.
> However Calypso has shuffled the marked pack, veiling with early the late.
> Through all unconformities and the sills without sequence,
> glorying all the under-dapple.

15 David Jones, *The Dying Gaul* (London: Faber and Faber, 1978), p. 142.

16 Julian of Norwich, *Revelations of Divine Love*, trans. by Clifton Wolters (Harmondsworth: Penguin Books, 1966), p. 68.

17 'If only the Geologists would let me alone, I could do very well, but those dreadful Hammers! I hear the sound of them at the end of every cadence of the Bible verses!' John Ruskin, letter to Henry Acland, 24 May 1851.

> Lighting the Cretaceous and the Trias, for Tyrannosaurus must somehow lie down with herbivores, or, the poet lied, which is not allowed.
> However violent the contortion or whatever the inversion of the folding.
> Oblique though the fire-wrought cold rock dyked from convulsions under.
> Through the slow sedimentations laid by his patient creature of water.
> . . .
> As, down among the palaeo-zoe
> he brights his ichthyic sign (*A*, p. 74)

In a passage such as this rhythm and language generate a sense of power. The effect is simultaneously to celebrate the material world and praise it as divinely created. We might describe this as a poetics of God's energy, a force manifested in 'the New Light' that shines with 'eternal clarities' in geological and biological processes. The Franciscan spirit is present 'through the slow sedimentations laid by his patient creature of water'. A humorous spirit also informs the poetry, in the reference to Calypso shuffling 'the marked pack', and in the updating of Isaiah: 'for Tyrannosaurus must somehow lie down with herbivores, or the poet lied, which is not allowed'. Here too Jones pays tribute to Gerard Manley Hopkins with 'glorying all the under-dapple'. Like Hopkins Jones has an acute sense of haeccity and inscape, as he shows in his use of geological terms as images, which are at once vital and significant: 'piercing the eskered silt, discovering every stria, each score and macula, lighting all the fragile laminae of the shales'. Word choice, patterns of sound, images, rhythm, all together generate an extraordinary sense of force: 'Oblique through the fire-wrought cold rock dyked from convulsions under'. Nothing except Hugh MacDiarmid's 'On a Raise Beach' comes close to engendering a similar sense of awe in modern British poetry. The difference from MacDiarmid is that Jones is an incarnational poet. As I have written elsewhere about passages such as this, 'the incarnational metaphysic marries an informing spiritual presence to rock-solid materiality'.[18] In this and similar passages alliterative word-sounds foreground not only individual words but also letters. This verbal art prefigures Jones's later painted inscriptions in which words and even letters stand out with the quality of things.

David Jones was primarily a maker whose aesthetics were rooted in theology. He discussed them in remarkable essays, such as 'Art and Sacrament' and 'Use and Sign'; and he embodied them in his writings and paintings. The integration of his thinking resulted at times in an extraordinary compression, as in his recalling of the prehistoric 'Master of the Venus':

18 Jeremy Hooker, *Imagining Wales*: A View of Modern Welsh Writing in English (Cardiff University of Wales Press, 2001), p. 125.

whose man-hands god-handled the Willendorf stone
before they unbound the last glaciation
for the Uhland Father to be-ribbon *die blaue Donau*
with his Vanabride blue.
O long before they lateen'd her Ister
or Romanitas manned her gender'd stream. (*A*, p. 59)

Words and images in the whole passage, of which this is only a fragment, have recession and depth: as Stuart Piggott said, 'the words are radio-active with history'.[19] Jones drew extensively on historical and geographical studies for his materials, and anthropology, archaeology, and philology were sciences that he found friendly to his purposes. His thought-world owed most to scholastic theology interpreted by Jacques Maritain, especially in the book, *Philosophy of Art*, which Jones read and reread after the war, in the early twenties. It was this that enabled a remarkable verbal and imagistic concentration, as in 'whose man-hands god-handled', which embodies a whole philosophy of sacramental art. Woman as source and inspiration of form and image making is seen in an historical context:

But already he's at it
the form-making proto-maker
busy at the fecund image of her.
Chthonic? why yes
but mother of us. (*A*, pp. 59 – 60)

The primeval process enacted by the 'Master of the Venus' finds its meaning in the Incarnation. Single words such as 'fecund' carry a world of meaning. The form-maker is busy at work upon the very source of human being: 'mother of us'.

Female creativity, representing all aspects of woman, and, in some sense, figuring the Mother of God, is a potent force in *The Anathemata*. Jones's writings are voiced; they are existential, bodily expressions of men and woman. John Ball and Dai are obvious examples in *In Parenthesis*. The voicing is dramatic, performative; and *The Anathemata* in particular gives voice to women.

The Lady of the Pool is a prime example – a persona who, no doubt, remembers David Jones's female relatives from Rotherhithe, garrulous old ladies whose voices contribute to a composite mythological figure who has known

19 Stuart Piggott, 'David Jones and the Past of Man', *Agenda* David Jones Special Issue, Vol. 5, Nos. 1-3, Spring-Summer, 1967, p. 78.

many ages and many lovers, and who has learned from them. Privy to learning, she has a vocabulary that draws on the Latin Mass and also includes words such as 'metaphysical' and 'phenomenology' and 'Sejunction'. As her name implies, she is identified closely with the river Thames, which she associates with 'a deal of subsidence':

> gravels, marls, alluviums
> here all's alluvial, cap'n, and as unstable as these old annals
> that do gravel us all. For, captain:
> even immolated kings
> be scarce a match for the deep fluvial doings of the mother. (*A*, p. 164)

Alluvial material includes both the actual geology on which London is founded and the 'old annals', including Arthurian myth. Both psychologically and culturally, the Lady voices Jones's principal hope that 'What's under works up'.

Here, we may intuit David Jones's own experience of Freudian analysis, which finally released him from a catastrophic depression and enabled him to work again. The subliminal is at work in this passage, with memories of the Blitz, and London blown open to reveal the past. The Second World War influenced the ethos of the poem, which was published only seven years after the war ended. *The Anathemata* issued into a world in which Hitler and Nazi territorial ambitions had been defeated, and London and many other major cities bore the cost of victory in scars left by the Blitz. In this context, the Lady says the unsayable:

> For should these stir, then would our Engle-raum in this
> Brut's Albion be like to come to some confusion! (*A*, p. 164)

In terms of David Jones's thought, the hope she expresses looks back to the 'Lord of Order' and forward to The Sleeping Lord', to the myth of Arthur, '*rexque futurus*', that represented his hope for the renewal of Christian civilization. The language of 'Engle-raum' is shocking. What makes it acceptable is Jones's love of England, and the fact that he was a Briton. When Jones invokes 'Brut's Albion' he is most like William Blake, who had said something similar to the English people of his time. Blake too had drawn attention to imaginative energies embodied in the landforms and the myths of the British Isles that could save the people from the oppression of a narrow English, imperial hegemony.

David Jones's writings, like James Joyce's, speak with the voices of common men and women. These are the poet's vehicles, which he adapts in making his 'shapes in words'. At the same time that he articulates a world of common experience he expresses a Christian ideal that is chivalric. This is mediated by his extensive use of Arthurian material and embodied in an Arthur who is a figure of Christ, 'the Eternal Victim' (*SL*, p. 80), 'the Lord of Order carrying a raid into the place of Chaos'. Here, again, the Franciscan link is strong. E. A. Armstrong refers to a remark recorded in *The Mirror of Perfection* that 'Francis as a youth had been inspired by the romances of King Arthur. He said of his friars: "These are my companions of the Round Table"'. Francis would say: 'We are the minstrels of the Lord', and he would ask: 'What are the Servants of the Lord but His minstrels, who should raise the hearts of men and move them to spiritual joy'.[20]

Does it make sense to think of David Jones as a 'minstrel of the Lord'? In considering him as a metaphysical poet we are suggesting more than a link between the modernist Jones and poets of the seventeenth century. A passage from 'The Book of Balaam's Ass' should make this clear. It begins by returning us to the world of *In Parenthesis*, with the voices of wounded soldiers, 'the half-cries of those who would call strongly from their several and lonely places, on/that Creature of Water, or on/some creature of their own kind'. The passage then moves into Jones's own voice, in theological mode:[21]

> On the Lamb because he was slain.
> On the Word seen by men because He was familiar with the wounding iron.
> On the Son of Man because He could not carry the cross-beam of his *stauros*.
> On the Son of Mary, because, like Perédur, He left His Mother to go for a soldier, for he would be a *miles* too.
> On Mary because of his secret piercing, and because, but for her pliant *Fiat mihi*, no womb-burden to joust with the fiend in the lists of Hierosolyma, in his fragile habergeon: HUMANA NATURA. (*SL*, pp. 107 – 108)

This passage has a naked quality – it is close to the liturgical voices that echo through his writings, but are seldom as overt as this. It includes a reference to Langland that is Jones's most explicit statement of his subject in all his poetry.

His images are incarnational; they unite the human and the divine. Jesus is Mary's 'womb-burden'. As Jones wrote in a letter to a friend: 'I suppose all my stuff has on the whole been central round the Queen of Heaven and cult-hero

20 Armstrong, *Saint Francis: Nature Mystic*, p. 21.

21 *Dai Greatcoat: a self-portrait of David Jones in his letters*, ed. by René Hague (London: Faber and Faber, 1980, p. 227.

– son and spouse'. His frequent Marian references celebrate Mary's willing submission to God's will and present her in womanly, bodily images, as a figure who suffers with her Son. Here, he uses a chivalric image of Christ jousting with the fiend, and alludes to Langland's use of a similar image. He quotes *Piers Plowman* 'B' Text:

> 'Is Piers in this place?' quod I, and he preynte on me.
> 'This Jesus of his gentries wol juste in Piers armes,
> In his helm and in his haubergeon – *humana naturata*.
> That Crist be noght biknowe here for *consummatus Deus,*
> In Piers paltok the Plowman this prikiere shal ryde.

> ('Is Piers in this city? I asked.
> He looked at me keenly and answered, 'Jesus, out of chivalry, will joust in Piers' coat-of-arms, and wear His helmet and mail, Human Nature: He will ride in Piers' doublet, that no one may know Him as Almighty God.)[22]

Jones wrote about Langland's B Text: '*What* a bloody good poem it is. Makes Chaucer, on the whole, lacking in *depth*, neither as "earthy" nor as "celestial"'.[23] The words 'earthy' and 'celestial' admirably define poetry that is 'creaturely yet other-world-ordered'. According to Jones's friend, Christopher Damson, the Catholic historian, Langland was 'the most remarkable and the most authentic representative of the religious sentiment of the common people of medieval England'.[24] Piers, Dawson says, is 'the type of Labour and Christian charity and at last of Christ himself'.[25] In this image of the Incarnation, Christ takes on Piers' armour – his Human Nature – to joust with 'the fiend'. Jones's Arthur, 'the Lord of Order carrying a raid into the place of Chaos' is essentially the same figure: type of a chivalric Christ transposed to the twentieth century. It is faith that links the modernist poet with his fourteenth-century predecessor.

Dawson describes Langland as 'a man in whom Catholic faith and national feeling are fused in a single flame'.[26] Something similar could be said of David

22 William Langland, *The Vision of Piers Plowman* Passus XVlll, 20-24, ed. by A. V. C. Schmidt (London: Dent Everyman's Library, 1987), p. 220. *Piers the Ploughman*, trans. by J. F. Goodridge (Harmondsworth: Penguin Books, 1959), p. 256.

23 Quoted in Dilworth, *David Jones Engraver, Soldier, Painter, Poet*, p. 288.

24 Christopher Dawson, *Medieval Essays*, 1954 (Washington DC: The Catholic University of America Press, n.d), p. 206.

25 Ibid., p. 216.

26 Ibid., p. 207.

Jones, providing we remember he was a Briton, not English in a narrow sense. Jones named the narrator of *In Parenthesis* John Ball, a name intended to recall the priest who led the Peasant's Revolt. The real John Ball quoted *Piers Plowman*, and we may infer that Jones had in mind the priest as a common man of faith. The subject of Langland's great poem was '*humana natura*', the nature that the incarnate Christ bore. Jones puts the words in capital letters: HUMAN NATURE. He could have given no clearer sign of what his work, like Langland's, affirms.

David Jones was a modernist. His principal modern influences were Gerard Manley Hopkins, *The Waste Land*, Joyce's *Ana Livia Plurabelle*, and *Anabase*, Eliot's translation of St John Perse's poem. While like other modernists he sought to keep open lines of communication between the present and the past, the main difficulty with which he struggled concerned the validity of religious signs in a utilitarian civilization. He subtitled *The Anathemata*, his greatest work 'fragments of an attempted writing', thus expressing his doubt that the kind of thing he wanted to make was any longer makeable. *The Anathemata* begins with priest and poet facing the same predicament: 'dead symbols litter to the base of the cult-stone'. (A, p. 50) The waste land metaphor he deploys in his writings – it as much setting as metaphor – represents ruin, disorder, chaos. It is, however, a metaphor that carries hope of restoration and renewal. Hope depends upon the asking of a question. Rather than presuming to answer the question, Jones's writings pose it in a form that reflects upon writer and reader:

> In this place of questioning where you must ask the question and the answer questions you.[27]

If the word metaphysical means anything when used to describe poetry, David Jones is clearly a metaphysical poet. His writings fulfil the definition of the seventeenth-century poets that he gave in his note. His work is 'creaturely yet other-world-ordered', 'ecstatical yet technically severe and ingenious, concerned with conditions of the psyche, but its images very much of the soma'. This is a suggestive definition, but it will not solve problems of seventeenth-century Metaphysical poetry as a disputed form. Literary critical terms help to define but should not be used to confine poetry. What I have tried to show may perhaps be summed up by Jones's use of the term 'counter-renaissant'.

What does he mean by this? The word 'ecstatical' may help us to understand. In the tradition espoused by Jones, which was strongly influenced by Scholastic philosophy, the artist is a maker who stands outside or alongside or

27 David Jones, *The Roman Quarry* and other sequences, ed. by Harman Grisewood and René Hague (London: Agenda Editions, 1981), p. 18.

above his work. The work is not about his subjective self. He partakes of the 'matter', but as a whole human being of flesh and blood and spirit, not a limited ego. We may recall that David Jones called his painted self-portrait *Human Being*. However learned he may be, however clever, a counter-renaissant poet is not Renaissance man, measure of all things. He is *humana natura*, a creature of 'the same world of sense as hairy ass and furry wolf', but 'who presumes to other and more radiant affinities'.

Jacques Maritain's *Art et Scholastique*, translated as *The Philosophy of Art*, and published at Ditchling in 1923, laid the foundations of Jones's aesthetic. The Renaissance, according to Maritain, 'shattered' the order of things that the Middle Ages knew:

> After three centuries of unbelief, prodigal art has made it her aim to be the last end of man, his Bread and Wine: the consubstantial mirror of beatific Beauty. In reality it has only wasted its substance. And the Poet starving for beatitude, who kept asking from art the mystical fullness which God alone can give, has merely emptied himself into the Sigean abyss. The silence of Rimbaud probably marks the end of a secular apostasy.[28]

In this view, the Renaissance originated 'a secular apostasy' that ended with the poet substituting art for God. Thomas Dilworth sums up Maritain's contention: 'that art is fundamentally sacramental, partly because every beauty emanates from God as primal Beauty. Making art is therefore a kind of prayer'.[29]

This was the philosophy of art to which David Jones subscribed in the years after the First World War, and to which he remained true lifelong. It was a philosophy that linked him not only to 'the English Metaphysicals' but also to Langland in the fourteenth century. It linked him also to the line of poets behind Langland – the Anglo-Saxons – poets with their roots in the Bible, in particular the New Testament and the Psalms. Jones found the tradition also in Arthurian Romance with its roots in immemorial religion, and in folksong, and in Samuel Johnson's friend, Christopher Smart, of whose *Jubilate Agno* Jones wrote: Smart 'prayed always in every line of his poem, for each line is a praise' (*E&A*, p. 280). Jones, like Smart and like the Metaphysical poets of the seventeenth century, was a poet of prayer and praise. Despite differences of historical period and style, all poets in this tradition share a common stance. They write not as beholders of life, but as participants, partakers of human nature. That is to say, they are sacramental or incarnational poets.

28 Jacques Maritain, *Philosophy of Art* (Ditchling, Sussex: S. Dominic's Press, 1923), p. 53.
29 Dilworth, *David Jones Engraver, Soldier, Painter, Poet*, p. 76.

LAURA POTTS

Jarrow Doll

These penitent nights, chapel-black
where the terrace turns its back to the hills,
after the wild white fists and the fight,
the blood-bite-kiss and the mist of the morning
over the dock, in the glowering grey
like a sentinel fox I slip in the dawn on

and beyond the wharfside-wetland-headland
away. Behind, my wound-tight sweat-damp
night and a lover whose name I never quite
know. Oh dockland dim and fog on the moor,
the wind at the water-bridge stops
at my corner-whore feet as I turn from that
frostshard street and home, a lone

lamp dim in the last laugh of night.
My Tyne-light mirrors me Madonna gone shy:
I who split spines of hills with my stride,
the mariner's wife who watched from the shore
that ship ten years too lost. Now, the frost
of my widowhood workhouse-dark, my skull
holding eyes like cradles carved

with a terminal hand, and then when
the river moves the moon through the land
and I hold something crèche in my canyon
again, to rinse off the men from my skin
I remember. Before the bairns get in, I am
a heavy, bleeding gender. Your medal tender
glows on from the hearth, man of my heart,
seaman my own. Know only this: though
the field sheds its coat to the wind your infants
are clothed in the sweet sweet spring of youth,
a matriarch lighthouse guiding them home.

JONATHAN WOODING

maker

the more I see of humanism the less I like it
Wallace Stevens to Hi Simons, January 9 1940

stay in your window-seat Wallace –
detect that force which outwits
nihilism, merely by gazing

tzaddik, hear the pilpul of bird sounds –
seelensfriede durch dichtung –
asides from woodwind's disbelief

there, tipped with ice, each sumac candle
is minded to give us back to ourselves
in a January mist not yet willing to rise

shadows longer than the longest tree,
the bramble-patch weighted with frost,
crocus clusters cluttering up

where grass is a shattered crystal vase –
between the sitter and the idling sun
points of blue, red, green light

are a scattered rainbow dispensed
by a cloudless, windless sky, casting
a spell for spathes of spring snowflakes

so the birds have it – their claim on mossed rubble,
valley's riverrun, oak leaves caught in pond ice,
and you, Wallace, just being human

Daleth/Adhaesit pavimento

cantos from *Psalm One Hundred and Nineteen*

My soul cleaveth to the dust

Vacancy is the door. The rood too
I've heard branded a gate, without success.
Even failure ails in our days,
as house-martins
cleave the air
in dextrorotation.

Soul-lights for me, anyway, African sky-divers,
cleaving the airs, also,
in laevorotation,
grounding our parliament of village fowls,
grounding them, so,
in cyclomorphosis!

The sundry and manifold changes of the world –
there for their hearts to be
fixed, too true,
no variableness, no shadow of turning,
and birdsong that cleaves
piercing AND catching.

Failure a lure this time, fathering lights –
even vacancy a door, and the rood a gate too.

Waw/Et veniat super me

cantos from *Psalm One Hundred and Nineteen*

Let thy loving mercy come also unto me, O Lord

This, Yeshua, is how God feels if you'll
pardon naked expressionism:
loving-kindness undone, you'll get nothing more than me.

Tyndale's dragon's a howler, a jackal
quenched as tow in the wolf of translation.
But hirondelles *cling to equality*, no doubt.

I play with *presurrection*, how'd you like it?
Before the day was I am he, like this:
planetary mist, ghosted half-moon, skein of flight.

Blossom still blasphemes its way timeously,
just oriflamme now in apple tree's tips.
And the truth is utterly out that you, Yeshua, fail.

Presurrection is yours, though, so far
as my canticle goes, so far as this.

Teth/Bonitatem fecisti

cantos from *Psalm One Hundred and Nineteen*

O Lord, thou hast dealt graciously with thy servant

Butterflies are happy for our garden.
Something coppery there, a small heath,
and a Wood White skipping, luciform.
A mistle-thrush, weather-beaten after storm,
dislodges an apple, our fálling dream.
I have not prepared for any of these events.

My mind is damaged goods, *teth's* broken wheel;
I *hack out of the quarry a small poem*
(Empson), and wonder at its *gīmaṭrĕyā.*

Faith vanishes at what's no longer hidden.
It's all there. The small heath, the wood white,
the weather-beaten mistle-thrush, her apple.

Time's a roulette wheel momently offering
dismay, even *a hoard of gold and silver.*

Yodh/Manus tuae fecerunt me

cantos from *Psalm One Hundred and Nineteen*

Thy hands have made me and fashioned me

It's the waiting. Waiting for the form
of a hand, in *likeness as the appearance*
of fire, from Ezekiel's amber chambers.

There in the nonsense, today, of my roustabout
apple trees and oak, the willow next door,
though not the form of a fiery, friendly hand.

It would all be too easy. There'd be no need
for Empson's *monstrously clotted* language –
antagonyms for faith which is affliction.

Swelling with the skittery breezes, willow
is no open hand but clutched then hurling,
yes, a likeness as the appearance of fire.

And, monstrously clotted, Ezekiel wavers
into afflicted speech, and this faithful, fiery hand.

BEATRICE TESSIER

New life

The cairn was once three metres high.
They took the stones away,
by hand, in trucks:
left the broken ones.

Then the rotting tree nearby
began to sprout
all up the trunk
lichens spread:
white, orange, green.

Who knew they grew that way
old souls starting afresh,
foliose, leprose, crustose.

Copper loch

Sometimes this loch reminds me of
a copper tea-tray purchased in
Aleppo's old souk.
See, Madam, the smith said,
how it ripples, how it glints,
I hammered it myself.
It is truly a magic tray, it echoes
with the sound of many gatherings,
it gives you pieces of what it sees,
in the morning it runs with the sun
in the evening moon-petals drift down,
it does not tarnish in the rain
but makes music,
it is thin yet has great depth,
it swarms with offerings;
Angels land on it, Madam,
sink their heads,
taste the forbidden fruit.

PAUL CONNOLLY

Dead Dog

The wind folds the skirts of his robe
back at himself, and then they billow

towards the dog he stares down
towards. Admiring its sleek perfection

he fears, though quelling with charms, its black
and death. A sudden nostrilled catch

of snort unveils the life. He considers
for a moment whether his power has resurrected it,

then it heaves into another choke. Should he
put it beyond pain? The destiny

of animals is fleshly durance. Their souls
only perdure truly in the throes

of my priestly dance. Shall I suck
its soul away now? He whacks

it with his staff. It spasms and shakes like an adept
shakes with Moon Brew. I must get

a stone. He drives the sharpened end
of a sulphur-coloured block through the head,

the eye whitens like a fish's on the fire,
the brain snots and livers. Awhile

he weeps, then walks away, then runs. Circumambient
howling, soft from the woods, is bent

on whichever point he occupies. Talk
and ceremony stifle the song, but when work

is done it comes again and spins
about his spinning head. The pains

of death gnaw at him one day.
Lying down on the priest stone, he prays

and feels his last feeling, the snout's
agonised birth stretch. He slavers and howls.

JOHN BARNIE

House Party

We discussed whether friends of ours would like one another
and, quite interested, the mountains listened in,
frost covered crags where weather was bent on production

of gravel and mud and whatever detritus
could be rushed in torrents to the tireless sea
to begin again the formation of rock, though not in our time;

I said, no, keep friends in boxes and bring them out
for your own enjoyment, don't mix gold with iron,
houses become kennels when there are too many dogs.

MIRIAM CRAIG

Jackdaws, the Lake District

I'm 33 and I've never really looked
at a bird in flight, the way it runs its wings
along the grain of breath.

Each bird makes separate hairpin turns,
just like the paths that weave
across the mountainside.

One pushes its wings back,
stretches out claws, presses a chord
into the earth, and lands.

They aren't the birds I copied
from after-school TV:
a lurid sunset, flocks of small black v's.

Those were from a much-used block,
gritty with being stamped
onto the mind.

Now I make pictures lie
flush with the world, because I've looked
at jackdaws with my own eyes.

REVIEWS

Elizabeth S. Dodd and Cassandra Gorman, eds, *Thomas Traherne and Seventeenth-Century Thought*. Suffolk and Rochester: Boydell and Brewer, 2016. ISBN 9781843844242. xx + 221 pp. Hb £60.00.

Thomas Traherne (*c*. 1637–1674) is a poet with a remarkable history of recovery in the last hundred years. But for a series of sometimes fortuitous manuscript discoveries between 1897 and 1996, he would be as little known today as he was in his own time. The first manuscript finds were originally attributed to Henry Vaughan, until Bertram Dobell identified Traherne as the author. Since the publication of the poems and *Centuries of Meditations* from the Dobell folio in 1903/1908, Traherne has been assured a place in literary history. The early reception of these works set the mould for interpreting him as a proto-romantic, visionary poet of innocence and childhood. Nevertheless, as Julia Smith points out in her fine prefatory overview of Traherne's critical fortunes, his poetry has been criticised as flawed, even inferior, for not fitting the inappropriate categories imposed on his writing. Another remarkable aspect of Traherne's twentieth-century reception is the way that the spiritual dimension of his poems and their stylistic accessibility has earned him a following, independently of the literary critics, as a poet who seems to speak directly to the present. This is amply illustrated by the annual festival held at Credenhill, Herefordshire, where he once was rector, which attracts a non-academic audience, including religious believers of many callings. However, further manuscript discoveries, most recently in 1996, show that there is far more to Traherne than can be accommodated by his twentieth century literary *persona*. Far from being some kind of reclusive primitive, the Traherne that emerges from the recently discovered notebooks and prose treatises, is someone fully engaged with the intellectual, ecclesiological and political context of his time. The volume under review is testimony to the liberating impact of those discoveries for re-evaluating Traherne as a writer. Elizabeth Dodd and Cassandra Gorman have assembled a collection of papers by contributors, drawn from English Studies or Theology, who collectively challenge the received orthodoxies. Each paper, in its own way offers a new perspective on Traherne the poet, in sometimes surprising ways. Three papers focus on the material themes in Traherne's writings, illustrating how much this most spiritual of poets was grounded physically in tangible 'thing-iness': Phoebe Dickerson on references to skin, and Cassandra Gorman on Traherne's fascination with atomism, and a superbly argued paper by Kathryn Murphy on Traherne's material realism, which highlights the relevance of Francis Bacon and the Royal Society. There are two studies of 'The Ceremonial Law', the unfinished, didactic religious poem from the Folger collection, one by Warren Chernaik and one by Carol Ann Johnston, both of which relate the poem to contemporary 'puritan' typological traditions. Two contributors revisit classic Traherne themes by exploring them in relation to contemporary devotional literature: Ana Elena González-Treviño on happiness and Elisabeth Dodd on innocence demonstrate just how studious Traherne was in pursuing these themes. Alison Kershaw tackles the too-often ignored subject of Traherne's theology, with a paper on his Christology.

A major difficulty for assessing Traherne in relation to seventeenth-century thought, as this volume aspires to do, is that there is no up-to-date overview of the intellectual context, never mind a joined-up one. The inter-regnum and Restoration tend to be treated separately, with their inter-tangled political, philosophical and religious history fragmented along confessional and disciplinary lines. Literary scholars rarely question the suitability of terms like 'puritan', 'radical', 'latitudinarian', and even what it meant to be an 'Anglican'. On the philosophical side, it is only relatively recently that Hobbes has been brought into the broader picture, while Platonism, so relevant to Traherne, is routinely mis-characterised as mysticism. It is perhaps indicative of the imperfect state of the intellectual history for this period that two contributors have reached forward to the present—Dickerson to Jean-Luc Nancy and Kershaw to Teilhard de Chardin—instead of to sources available at the time, for example Nicholas of Cusa and Origen for Traherne's cosmic Christ. The omission of Henry More's *Democritus platonissans* from Cassandra Gorman's discussion of poetic atomism is puzzling. Carol Ann Johnston rightly attempts a new look at Traherne's religious and political loyalties, but it does not seem to me that this is a question that can be settled by typology alone. The theology underlining divisions among Calvinists, Presbyterians and Independents, is crucial here. Perhaps Traherne's 'Sober View' of the Calvinist predestinarian, William Twisse, might shed some light. A suggestive reference to Peter Sterry in Professor Johnston's paper might be pursued through to the other Cambridge Platonists and to a consideration of Traherne's patronage networks. His last employer, Orlando Bridgman, was a colleague of Heneage Finch, patron of More and Cudworth. For these reasons, it is too early to claim, as Jacob Blevins does in his afterword, that this collection 'marks the culmination, the climax, of our new understanding of Traherne's place in seventeenth century thought'. But it takes a decisive a step in that direction.

Sarah Hutton
Honorary Visiting Professor, University of York

Elizabeth Siberry and Robert Wilcher, eds, *Henry Vaughan and the Usk Valley*. Logaston, Herefordshire: Logaston Press, 2016. ISBN: 978 1 910839 02 7. xviii + 110 pp. Hb £10.00.

The small, delightful volume, *Henry Vaughan and the Usk Valley*, jointly commissioned by the Brecknock Society and the Vaughan Association, could be compared, in George Herbert's words, to a 'box, where sweets compacted lie.' As readers turn the richly illustrated pages, where pride of place is given to fully cited poems, they are taken on a walk through Vaughan's poetic oeuvre, along the bucolic paths of Llansantffraed the poet himself trod centuries back, to the foot of the Silurist's 'curtained grave' ('The Morning-Watch', cited p. 56). Though the book is avowedly hagiographic in design, setting off to 'celebrate [Vaughan's] life and work' (p. vii), to promote his poetry to a broader public, and to encourage visits to his native landscapes, this purpose does not detract from its scholarly insightfulness. The chapters, by some of today's greatest specialists of Vaughan's writings, follow a loosely chronological structure. After the introductory biographical sketch, chapter 1 by Jeremy Hooker seeks to root Vaughan in the 'sacred' brooks, valleys, trees and ground of Brecknockshire while acknowledging that Vaughan was not a 'local poet' nor one with an 'eye for topographical detail' (p. 4). Vaughan's open gaze and 'fascination with water and light' betray, rather, the general radiance of the Welsh landscape upon his imagination, turning the local terrain into Holy Land, and space into 'Presence' in ways that show an affinity between his poetry and 'the medieval Dafydd ap Gwilym's sanctification of the greenwood' (p. 9). Robert Wilcher's second chapter, devoted to the dark days of the Civil Wars and a breach in this sense of sacred place and the happy early education of the poet, yields a sharp and moving portrait of Vaughan as a soldier. Wilcher turns to facets of Vaughan's character and work that have received too little critical attention. The chapter highlights the poet's political and satirical vein in such poems as 'To His Retired Friend' or 'The King Disguised', troublingly poised between the acknowledgment of the 'demeaning' of the king's 'sacred person' and an attempt to 'salvage something of the mystique of kingship' (p. 22). The unexpected attention to the material details of war in elegies for lost friends or 'Upon a Cloak Lent Him by Mr J. Ridsley' suddenly touches Vaughan with the same thickness and reality we are used to attributing to war poets of more recent times. In chapter 3, Wilcher goes on to explore Vaughan's poetic and professional activities during the Interregnum, not only his quest for comfort, as voiced in *Solitudis Flores* and *Silex Scintillans*, but also the expression of his 'fierce soul' ('Misery'), which resented the religious consequences of 'Puritan dominance' (p. 38) and resisted 'the meekness and forgiveness demanded of him as a Christian' (p. 36). Helen Wilcox reconciles Vaughan with the more peaceful image of the Christian poet in the following chapter (4). She concentrates on his deep and inward relation to a Church which, though forced into invisible existence, was not extinguished altogether. Renewing in slightly different terms L. L. Martz's seminal thesis of a 'paradise within', she devotes her attention to Vaughan's 'compensatory spiritual activity' (p. 49), even while she shows the poet walking through the '*waste and howling Wildernesse*' ('Dedication' to *The Mount of Olives*) of the 'Cavalier Winter'. Chapters 5, '"The truth and light of things': Henry Vaughan and Nature' by Jonathan Nauman, and 6, '"New

Corials, New Cathartics": Henry Vaughan the Physician' by Simone Thomas, deepen the exploration of Vaughan's engagement with nature, as both a physical and a metaphysical entity. Nauman carefully distinguishes between the characteristically Vaughnian 'sacred incubation' of the divine in nature, from vitalist hermetic and cabbalistic theories, or even later Romantic attitudes towards nature. An investigation of Vaughan's rich and eclectic medical library leads Simone Thomas to shed light upon the poet's interest in natural wonders and the 'signatures of plants' (p. 82). The book concludes with a seventh chapter by Elisabeth Siberry, dedicated to 'The Vaughan Heritage'. Siberry explores the instrumental work of the independent scholar Louise Guiney among others in the revival of the poet's memory at the end of the nineteenth-century and beginning of the twentieth, and invites readers to follow in Guiney's footsteps. There are no faults to be found in this beautiful publication, which amply fulfils its stated purpose of making Vaughan more accessible to the general public while providing glimpses into the best of scholarship on the Silurist's work. The authors' discreet erudition (few notes, all relegated to an end position) allows the readers to walk, as it were, through the pastoral environs of Llansantffraed, Tretower and the Usk Valley, while becoming immersed in the music of Vaughan's exquisite verse. Yet it also quietly calls attention to the many full-scale monographs that still lie waiting to be written on a great, yet relatively neglected author, when compared with other 'metaphysical poets'. The forthcoming Oxford edition of Vaughan's works edited by Donald R. Dickson, Alan Rudrum, and Robert Wilcher will certainly pave the way for the fuller revival that *Henry Vaughan and the Usk Valley* invites.

Anne-Marie Miller-Blaise
Université Sorbonne Nouvelle – Paris 3, EA PRISMES

Achsah Guibbory, *Returning to Donne*, Farnham, England, Ashgate Publishing Limited, 2015. ISBN: 9781409468783. ix + 268 pp. Hb £65.00.

Achsah Guibbory's new book gathers ten essays she published on Donne in various journals and edited collections over the course of her career, along with three new chapters. Some of these essays appeared in volumes no longer in print, and so their reappearance now is welcome, given Guibbory's stature as one of the most important interpreters of Donne since the early 1980s. But apart from convenience, this book additionally invites Guibbory to offer her readings of Donne as a cohesive whole. She makes the most of this opportunity. The essays are arranged not chronologically but in three topical sections: 'Time and History', 'Love', and 'Religion'. Every chapter contains riches galore, especially for those interested in metaphysical poetry, seventeenth-century religion, or both. But the value of the book derives also from Guibbory's honest reflections on the evolution of her thought over the past thirty years. Such retrospectives are all-too-rare in early modern scholarship. Readers of Vaughan will find especially intriguing Guibbory's sustained arguments that Donne was more Arminian than Calvinist in his theology after the accession of Charles I to the throne.

The book begins with a new chapter, '"Figuring Things Out": Donne's *Devotions Upon Emergent Occasions*', on how Donne's *Devotions*, his devotional account of his life-threatening bout of typhus in December 1623, examines the body as a means of understanding the soul and of finding solace in the face of what seemed impending death. Donne's perceptions of the entanglement of the physical and the spiritual, desire and fear, and society and the individual soul frame lively concerns in the essays that follow.

Each of the three ensuing sections begins with a fascinating account of Guibbory's intellectual development during the period when the essays were written, so that readers can chart the development of her ideas over time. Throughout, Guibbory writes clearly and personably and takes care to confess the circumstances that contributed to the genesis of certain insights—without shifting undue attention away from her subjects at hand. Often enough she provides brief biographical context in the essays themselves. When speaking of the connection between the *Songs and Sonets* and the *Song of Songs*, for example, she says it 'first struck me when in preparing a memorial service for a close friend (a poet in her own right) I came across a passage in the biblical *Song* that seemed a clue to Donne's enigmatic poem "The Relique"' (chapter 7, 125). Such disclosures make her writing refreshing to read. They acknowledge how scholarship issues from lived experience, like poems.

The first section, 'Time and History', establishes Guibbory's abiding interest in the power of historical, intellectual, and cultural recovery. Yet unlike some new historicist scholarship, Guibbory never treats Donne's writings strictly as cultural products but as the expression of a distinctive person, writing out of his historical moment. Chapter 2, 'John Donne: The Idea of Decay', which analyzes Donne's treatment of history, shows how memory for Donne acts as a personal remedy for an otherwise overwhelming sense of helplessness. In chapter 3, Guibbory compares Donne's and Jonson's belief that poetry is capable of generating a kind of earthly immortality when it finds readers years or even ages hence, though Jonson seems to have been more taken with this idea than Donne.

The second section, 'Love', includes six chapters on Donne's *Elegies*, *Songs and Sonets*, and *Divine Poems*, considered within the contexts of coterie poetry, Donne's lifelong interest in religion, and his relationship with his wife Anne. Chapter 4 establishes the complexity of Donne's perspectives on love in his work as a whole. Chapter 5, '"Oh, Let Mee Not Serve So': The Politics of Love in Donne's Elegies', which received the Distinguished Publication Award from the John Donne Society in 1990, is Guibbory's landmark analysis of misogyny in Donne's *Elegies*. Rather than treat the poems exclusively as coded expressions of political concerns, Guibbory argues that Donne's exploration of desire and gender hierarchies is itself political, and that the *Elegies* suggest Donne, like other Inns of Court contemporaries, bristled at the seeming disruptions of gender hierarchies as a result of Elizabeth I's rule. Turning to Donne's more variegated representation of love in the *Songs and Sonets*, chapter 6, 'Donne, Milton, and Holy Sex,' explores how Donne's lyrics and Book IV of *Paradise Lost* similarly represent sex as sacred when it issues from a truly mutual love. Milton could have found in Donne a 'poetic precedent' for his celebration of the holiness of sex in the Garden of Eden (109). Positioned as a continuation of Donne's celebration of erotic love, chapter 7 contends that in writing 'The Relique'—as well as the mutual love poems in the *Songs and Sonets* generally—Donne, whose Hebrew may have been better than his Greek, was inspired by the *Song of Songs*, not as it was re-imagined in various Christian Bibles but in its earlier untampered Hebrew version. Not only does 'The Relique' share several clusters of images with the Hebrew text but also it (mostly) eschews the Pauline dualism between flesh and spirit that would posit sex as a disordered, corrupt act. There follows 'Fear of "loving More": Death and the Loss of Sacramental Love,' Guibbory's elucidation of Donne's poetic responses to the loss of mutual love after the untimely death of Anne in 1617. What happens when such love is snatched away? Guibbory asks. She sees in four late poems evidence that Anne's death resulted in a 'kind of crisis of faith' in Donne's understanding of human love. A new essay, 'Depersonalization, Disappointment, and Disillusion', concludes this section by reminding us that as much as some of Donne's love poems celebrate spiritual completion through 'holy sex', others air the darker implications of post-coital tristesse.

The last section of the book, 'Religion', might be the most immediately of interest to readers of Vaughan. Here Guibbory makes her case that Donne, like Richard Montagu and other members of the church hierarchy, was 'an Arminian in theology' during the late 1620s, 'embracing and promoting a liberal, universalist (anti-Calvinist) view of grace', and that this view helped him to maintain a connection with his Catholic family heritage—or at least find some consolation about the ultimate fate of his recusant forebears (179). Chapter 10, 'Donne's Religion: Montague, Arminianism, and Donne's Sermons, 1624-1630', presents this argument in full, citing parallels between Donne's sermons and Montagu's *A Gagg for the new Gospel?* (1624) and *Appello Caesarem* (1625), to suggest that during his last years as Dean of St. Paul's Cathedral, Donne adopted a capacious understanding of grace, human free will, and the breadth of divine mercy more in consonance with English Arminianism than the orthodox Calvinism of George

Abbott. This is a controversial argument, given the assiduousness with which some scholars writing on the sermons insist on Donne's commitment to a 'moderate Calvinism' throughout his priestly years. But the evidence that Guibbory marshals is persuasive, and this essay should receive a wide reading. This is not to say, however, that Donne easily fits into any specific confessional label if we consider his work as a whole. The following chapter, 'Donne's Religious Poetry and the Trauma of Grace', demonstrates that Donne's religious poems, written long before the late sermons and from the vantage of a community outsider, repeatedly explore the 'trauma of grace' that can ensue from the Calvinist doctrine of double predestination. Vaughan, too, wrote as a forced outsider during the years of his greatest literary productivity (1648-1655), and so Guibbory's account offers grounds for an implicit contrast of the two poet's responses to spiritual turmoil. In chapter 12, 'Donne and Apostasy', Guibbory usefully summarizes the controversy over how we label Donne's shift from the Catholicism of his youth to his eventual ordination in the Established Stuart Church. Taking issue with the simplistic labeling of Donne as an apostate, she highlights the fluidity of religious identities in this period and discusses the frequency with which Donne himself explores issues of faithfulness, change, and conversion. The final chapter, 'Donne, Milton, Spinoza and Toleration: A Cross-Confessional Perspective,' another new contribution, nicely closes both the section and the volume by situating Donne's evolving understanding of religion within a select history of religious toleration. Guibbory finds striking parallels between Donne and Baruch Spinoza later in the seventeenth century. Donne's criticism of the control of religious and secular authorities over the individual conscience in 'Satire III' and his implicit criticism of the exclusionary tendencies of Calvinism in his late sermons accord with Spinoza's similar attacks on Calvinist intolerance in his *Tractus Theologico-Politicus* (1670). In this reading, Donne anticipates certain key ideas that greatly informed conceptions of toleration in the later seventeenth and eighteenth centuries. Vaughan's experience of Puritan intolerance likely colored his understanding of toleration. Yet the grounds of both Donne's and Spinoza's critiques of Calvinism likely would have appealed to him.

Overall, the Donne who emerges in these pages is complex, passionate, and bold, perennially engaged in questions of human and divine love and immersed in the hazardous negotiations between the individual, society, and the Christian afterlife—a man not perfect yet not rooted in his imperfections either, a perpetual seeker unafraid of pushing limits but savvy enough to participate effectively in the public sphere, a work-in-progress who was in some ways ahead of his time. Guibbory's reading of Donne is remarkably consistent and continually insightful. As a result, *Returning to Donne* makes a significant contribution to seventeenth-century studies. It also is a generous exercise in the value of taking an honest, retrospective look at one's own work.

Sean H. McDowell
Seattle University

CONTRIBUTORS

MARIA APICHELLA's debut *Psalmody* (Eyewear) was shortlisted for the First Collection Forward Prize, 2017 and Wales Book of the Year. *Paga* was published by Cinnamon Press (2015). She studied Creative Writing in Aberystwyth, Wales.

JOHN BARNIE is a poet and essayist. He edited the Welsh cultural magazine *Planet* from 1990-2006. Throughout 2016 he was one of three poets in residence at the Museum of Natural History, Oxford. His latest book is a collection of poems, *Departure Lounge* (Cinnamon Press, 2018).

MATTHEW BARTON's latest collection is *Family Tree*, Shoestring Press 2016. He is also the editor of *Raceme* poetry magazine.

PAUL CONNOLLY's poems have been published in *Agenda*, *The Warwick Review*, *Poetry Salzburg Review*, *The Reader*, *The Journal*, *Dream Catcher*, *Orbis*, *Cannon's Mouth*, *The Dawntreader*, and the inaugural edition of *Canada Quarterly*. He was shortlisted for the Bridport Prize and awarded Third Prize in the Magna Carta Poetry Competition.

MIRIAM CRAIG is a children's writer based in London. Her poetry has appeared in *Obsessed With Pipework* and she was part of the writing team who created *My Golden Ticket*, a children's book published by start-up Wonderbly in conjunction with the Roald Dahl Estate.

PATRICK DEELEY is from Loughrea, County Galway, Ireland. His poems have won many awards and been published and translated widely over the past forty years. *Groundswell: New and Selected Poems* is the latest with Dedalus Press. *The Hurley Maker's Son* (2016), was published by Transworld.

CAROL DEVAUGHN is an American-born poet living in London. She has won several poetry prizes, including a Bridport in 2012. Her work has been published in magazines, anthologies, and on-line. She has been reciting poems for charity since 1995.

K.E. DUFFIN's work has appeared in *Abridged*, *Agenda*, *Agni*, *Carolina Quarterly*, *The Cincinnati Review*, *Crannóg*, *Harvard Review*, *Kestrel*, *The Moth*, *Ploughshares Poetry*, *Poetry Salzburg Review*, *Prairie Schooner*, *Scintilla* (18), *The Sewanee Review Shenandoah*, *The SHOp*, *Southern Poetry Review*, *Thrush*, *Verse*, and other journals.

MICHAEL DURRANT is Lecturer in Early Modern Literature at Bangor University. His first book, which focuses on the life and career of the seventeenth century printer-publisher, Henry Hills, will be published by Manchester University Press in 2019.

ROSE FLINT is a poet and art therapist living in Wiltshire. She has five collections, most recently 'A Prism for the Sun, from Oversteps. A previous winner of the Cardiff International Poetry Prize and the Petra Kenney Internation Prize. She works with a multi-arts team in Salisbury Hospital.

JOHN FREEMAN's *What Possessed Me* (Worple Press, 2016) won the Roland Mathias Poetry Award as part of the Wales Book of the Year Awards, 2017. *Strata Smith and the Anthropocene* (Knives Forks and Spoons Press) appeared 2016, and earlier *A Suite for Summer* (Worple), *White Wings: New and Selected Prose Poems* (Contraband Books), and *The Light Is Of Love, I Think: New and Selected Poems* (Stride Editions).

ROGER GARFITT lives in the Shropshire Hills. His *Selected Poems* is published by Carcanet. A new collection, *The Action*, is forthcoming. *In All My Holy Mountain*, a Celebration in Poetry & Jazz of the life and work of Mary Webb, with jazz composer Nikki Iles and the John Williams Octet, is available from www.jazzcds.co.uk.

PHILIP GROSS has published twenty collections of poetry, including *A Bright Acoustic* (Bloodaxe, 2017). *The Water Table* (T.S. Eliot Prize 2009), and *Love Songs of Carbon* (Roland Mathias Award, Wales Book of The Year, 2016). He has collaborated with artist Valerie Coffin Price on *A Fold In The River* (Seren, 2015) and Australian poet-artist, Jenny Pollak, on *Shadowplay* (Flarestack, 2018).

ALYSON HALLETT's latest pamphlet, *Toots*, was shortlisted for the 2017 Michael Marks Award. Other books include *Limping Stumbling Walking Falling* (Triarchy Press), *Geographical Intimacy* (Amazon), *Suddenly Everything* (Poetry Salzburg), *The Stone Library* (Peterloo Poets) and *The Heart's Elliptical Orbit* (Solidus Press). www.thestonelibrary.com

JOHN HAYNES won the Costa Prize 2006 for *Letter to Patience (Seren)*. He was shortlisted for the 2010 T.S. Eliot Prize for *You (Seren), and* won the 2007 Troubadour Prize. He lectured in Nigeria for eighteen years. The poems here come from *Accompanying*, in memory of his seaside showbiz parents.

JEREMY HOOKER's most recent publications are *Ditch Vision: Essays on Poetry, Nature, and Place* (Awen, 2017), and a sequence of prose poems, *Under the Quarry Woods* (Pottery Press, 2018). He has completed a new collection of poems (*Word and Stone*), and is finishing a book of essays on poetry, painting, and photography (*Art of Seeing*). He is an emeritus professor of the University of South Wales.

ROSIE JACKSON is a prize-winning poet and Hawthornden fellow. *The Light Box* (Cultured Llama, 2016) followed *What the Ground Holds* (Poetry Salzburg, 2014). Prose books include *Fantasy: The Literature of Subversion; Frieda Lawrence; Mothers Who Leave* and a memoir *The Glass Mother* (Unthank Books, 2016).
www.rosiejackson.org.uk

W.D. JACKSON lives in Munich. His books of poetry *Then and Now – Words in the Dark* and *From Now to Then* are published by Menard Press and *Boccaccio in Florence* by Shearsman. *Afterwords* appeared from Shoestring in 2014, and *Opus 3* is due from the same publisher later this year.

EITHNE LANNON is a native of Dublin, Ireland.. She has been included in publications such as *The Ogham Stone, Boyne Berries, Skylight 47* and *FLARE*. Online she has had work published with Headstuff, Bare Hands, Sheila-na-Gig, *Artis Natura,* BeZine and A New Ulster.

PAUL MATTHEWS teaches at Emerson College in Sussex. His books, 'Sing Me the Creation', and 'Words in Place' (Hawthorn Press) explore the relationship between word and world. 'The Ground that Love Seeks' and 'Slippery Characters' (Five Seasons Press) are gatherings of his poetry. Another, 'This Naked Light' is forthcoming.
www.paulmatthewspoetry.co.uk

SEAN H. MCDOWELL is Director of University Honors and Associate Professor of English and Creative Writing at Seattle University. He has published a variety of essays on Shakespeare, Donne, Vaughan, George Herbert, Richard Crashaw, Andrew Marvell, and others, including Irish poets Tony Curtis and Seamus Heaney. A textual editor and commentary editor for *The Variorum Edition of the Poetry of John Donne*, he also edits *John Donne Journal: Studies in the Age of Donne.*

CHRISTOPHER MEREDITH is a novelist, poet and translator and is Emeritus Professor of Creative Writing at the University of South Wales. He was born in Tredegar and lives in Brecon. Novels include *Shifts* and *The Book of Idiots*. His recent poetry collection is *Air Histories*. *Brief Lives – six fictions*, will be published by Seren in June 2018.

PETE MULLINEAUX lives in Galway, Ireland, and works in development education. He teaches creative writing through poetry and drama. He has four collections: *Zen Traffic Lights* (Lapwing 2005), *A Father's Day* (Salmon 2008), *Session* (Salmon 2011), and *How to Bake a Planet* (Salmon 2016). He's also had a number of plays produced for Irish national radio.

NICHOLAS MURRAY's latest poetry collection is *The Museum of Truth* (Melos). His *Crossings: a journey through borders* was published in 2016 by Seren. He is a poet and literary biographer and lives in the Welsh Marches where he runs Rack Press Poetry with his wife Susan Murray.

ALAN PAYNE was born in Trinidad and lives in Sheffield. His pamphlet *Exploring the Orinoco* won the Poetry Business competition (2009-10). His poems are published in *Smiths Knoll*, *The North* and *Scintilla*, and anthologies including *The Sheffield Anthology: Poems from the City Imagined.*

JAMES PEAKE was born in Wimbledon and educated at Bristol University and Trinity College, Dublin. His poems have appeared in numerous anthologies and magazines including *Horizon*, *shadowtrain*, *The Reader*, *Poetry Salzburg Review*, Eyewear's *Best of British and Irish Poets 2017* and *The Next Review.*

LAURA POTTS, a twice-named Foyle Young Poet of the Year, lives in West Yorkshire. She was last year shortlisted in The Oxford Brookes International Poetry Prize and nominated for a Pushcart Prize. She also became one of The Poetry Business' New Poets and a BBC New Voice for 2017. In 2018 she received a commendation from The Poetry Society.

CHRIS PREDDLE has a third collection, *The May Figures*, coming from Eyewear in summer 2018. His second collection was *Cattle Console Him* (Waywiser, 2010). He has retired from library work to the Holme Valley in West Yorkshire, beside Mag Brook. He is translating the songs and fragments of Sappho.

RICKY RAY edits the journal *Rascal*. His debut collection is forthcoming from Eyewear (2018). He won the Fortnight Poetry Prize, the Ron McFarland Poetry Prize and the Cormac McCarthy Prize. He lives in Manhattan with his wife, three cats and a Labradetter. See rickyray.co

K.V. SKENE's poetry has appeared internationally. Her most recent publications include *Love in the (Irrational) Imperfect*, Hidden Brook Press (2006), *You Can Almost Hear Their Voices*, Indigo Dreams Publishing (2010) and *Under Aristotle Bridge,* Finishing Line Press (2015). KV currently writes and lives in Toronto, Canada.

BEATRICE TEISSIER is an archaeologist and independent scholar. She has recently completed an M. Phil in writing from the University of South Wales.

SUSAN WALLACE is an author and academic. She enjoyed writing poetry in her less than scandalous youth and, after becoming distracted by other things, eventually found her way back to it. As well as presenting at poetry readings and other literary events, she has had her work published in a number of anthologies and national journals.

ROBERT WILCHER was Reader in Early Modern Studies at the University of Birmingham and is now an honorary Fellow of the Shakespeare Institute. His publications include *Andrew Marvell* (CUP, 1985), *The Writing of Royalism 1628-1660* (CUP, 2001), *The Discontented Cavalier: The Work of Sir John Suckling in its Social, Religious, Political, and Literary Contexts* (University of Delaware Press, 2007), and articles on seventeenth-century poetry. He edited *Henry Vaughan and the Usk Valley* (Logaston Press) with

Elizabeth Siberry and is co-editor of a new complete works of Henry Vaughan to be published by Oxford University Press in 2018.

DR ROWAN WILLIAMS, born in South Wales, was Professor of Divinity at Oxford (1986-91), Bishop of Monmouth (1991-1999) and Archbishop of Wales (1999-2002) before becoming Archbishop of Canterbury – the first Welsh bishop to hold that office since the Reformation. On his retirement from Canterbury in 2012 he was made Baron Williams of Oystermouth. Lord Williams is currently Master of Magdalene College, Cambridge, and is internationally known as a theologian, poet, speaker and writer. Among his most recent books are *Being Christian* (2014), *Being Disciples* (2016), *On Augustine* (2016) and *Holy Living: The Christian Tradition for Today* (2017).

CHARLES WILKINSON's work includes a pamphlet, *Ag & Au*, from Flarestack Poets. *The Glazier's Choice,* is forthcoming from Eyewear (2018). *A Twist in the Eye*, his collection of weird fiction and strange tales, appeared from Egaeus Press (2016); a second book will appear from the same publisher in the near future. He lives in Powys, Wales.

JONATHAN WOODING, an Anglican Quaker and Friend of St Beuno's, writes on prayer and the post-religious condition. His doctorate – *Natural Strange Beatitudes* – was awarded for a poetry collection, *An Atheist's Prayer Book* and a study of Geoffrey Hill's *The Orchards of Syon*. Currently researching prophetic voice in Hill's 'The Daybooks'.

FEATURED ARTIST
TANJA BUTLER

TANJA BUTLER is a painter, printmaker and liturgical artist whose studio is located near Albany, NY. Her work is included in the collections of the Vatican Museum of Contemporary Religious Art, the Armand Hammer Collection of Art in Los Angeles, the Portland Museum of Art in Maine, the DeCordova Museum in Lincoln MA, and the Boston Public Library. Her subjects are devotional in nature. She enjoys working collaboratively to create liturgical art for specific worship environments. Byzantine icons, American and European folk art, Persian manuscripts, and Expressionist paintings are sources of inspiration. Samples of her work can be seen at www.tanjabutler.com.

Printed in Great Britain
by Amazon